True Real Life Stories Of Reincarnation

Amazing Past Life Memories

Compendium Contains:

Book One: True Real Life Stories Of Reincarnation

Book Two: 12 Real Life Reincarnation Stories In The News

Richard Bullivant

All Rights Reserved. No part of this publication may be reproduced in any form or by any means, including scanning, photocopying, or otherwise without prior written permission of Richard Bullivant.
Copyright © 2015

Book One

True Real Life Stories Of Reincarnation

Amazing Past Life Memories

Contents

Book One iii

Introduction 7

Bentreshyt – A Priestess of Isis 11

The Reawakening of Marty Martin 21

Past Lives on Other Planets.. 31

The Interesting Case of Sherrie Lea Laird and Marilyn 39

Life on Mars 49

Group Reincarnation 61

The Druze 71

The Genius Connection 81

The Science of Reincarnation 91

Future-Life Reincarnation 101

Book Two 115

Introduction 119

Dr Paul DeBell – Past Life Regression Therapy 123

Jeffrey Keene & The Civil War General 129

Samuel Helander & His Uncle Pertti 135

The Amazing Case of Uttara Huddar & Xenoglossy 141

Life Between Life 155

Split Reincarnation – One Soul, Many Lives 161

The British Carl Edon & The German Heinrich Richter 167

Suicide and Reincarnation 171

Maroczy (Deceased) v Korchnoi (Living) Chess Match 1985 177

Dolores Jay – Suggested Reincarnation? 185

The Spirit Guides 191

Conclusion 197

Introduction

Just a few years ago most stories about reincarnation were obscure tales that came to us from remote villages in India.

Now and then a modern western newspaper reporter would travel to the East and return with a remarkable tale about a Hindu boy or girl who had recalled a past life.

The story is always more or less the same. It plays out this way:

A child inexplicably begins to speak of the 'person I used to be'. He remembers living in a different village, eating different foods, living at a higher or lower economic level, and so on. He may even remember his former name, or the name of his wife. The parents, if only to allay the distress of the child, decide to investigate.

Lo and behold, they visit a nearby village and locate the exact house where the child said he used to live. They meet his former relatives, spouse, and his old neighbours. The child reels off a series of remarkable facts about the life of the deceased, most of which can be verified – it seems obvious that a bona fide case of reincarnation has been uncovered!

Whilst fascinating, just about all of these stories were easy to dismiss.

First of all, most of these tales seem to come from obscure locations deep within the Indian continent. Initially, because people in modern nations held preconceived notions about 'Hindu mysticism', it was easy to write off these stories as being the product of cultural biases and arcane belief systems.

But things began to change.

In the late 19th Century and early 20th Century Great Britain, the topic of reincarnation was infused with renewed interest as occult groups such as Madame Blavatsky's Theosophy emerged. Other more scientific groups, such as the British Society for Psychical Research founded in 1882, brought together cutting edge thinkers who were at least willing to look at paranormal phenomena which most scientists considered outside the realm of mainstream science.

So, beginning about one hundred years ago, the idea of reincarnation was at least partially brought out of the mysterious depths of ancient India and into at least some segments of the Western mindset – although belief in reincarnation remained well on the fringe.

Then in 1952, a remarkable story emerged from a small town in the American state of Colorado called Pueblo. A businessman who was from this area was dabbling in hypnotism as a hobby and decided to put a local housewife in a trance. His goal was to alleviate her persistent headaches.

The businessman, Morey Bernstein, was in for the surprise of his life when his subject, Virginia Tighe, spontaneously began to speak of a past life in Ireland. The woman believed she had been a little Irish girl by the name of Bridey Murphy who had lived in Cork in the year 1806. What followed was a detailed description of an entire life lived thousands of miles away and in a previous century.

When a local newspaper got hold of the story, the result was a sensation. The original article was soon picked up by major media outlets around the globe, and a book was eventually published. The book was followed by a Hollywood movie.

Suddenly the idea of reincarnation had gripped the rank-and-file American middle class. There was just something about the story that produced a wave of resonance within the consciousness of modern society. It seemed to have struck a chord.

The Bridey Murphy case also became extremely controversial. Sceptical investigators travelled to Cork and found dozens of inconsistencies with the facts of the life of Bridey Murphy as told by Colorado housewife Virginia Tighe.

Tighe herself would later say the whole situation ruined her life. The media attention, the virulent negative criticism, the accusations of mental instability - all of it took a toll on what had once been the normal happy life of a small-town American housewife.

However, what even the harshest critics and sceptics of the Bridey Murphy case did not understand was this: It proved that a modern audience was not only ready to confront the possibility of reincarnation, but that there was something about the story that gripped imaginations in a way that was more than mere sensation.

It seemed like the time had come for an awakening - or perhaps a reawakening. It was almost as if the idea of reincarnation had been buried in the subconscious minds of everyone all along - that is, it had been stamped down and pushed aside by modern science but now this concept was eager to burst forward again.

Today, hardly a week goes by when there is not a story of reincarnation presented in any given newspaper in any given country around the world. Furthermore, stories of reincarnation are carried by the most respected and venerable of mainstream newspapers, not just sleazy tabloids.

The growing number of new and exciting cases of reincarnation covered in today's modern media is the inspiration for this book. We will be taking a deeper look at some of the most intriguing stories taken from recent headlines. Our survey of major newspapers around the world reveal not only amazing personal stories of people who say they have been reincarnated, but it demonstrates what appears to be a growing public acceptance of the possibility that all of us will live again after we finish our present 'go-around' on the planet Earth.

What's even more intriguing is that cutting edge science truly seems to be getting on board.

No segment of society has held the idea of reincarnation in greater contempt than has the scientific community but, as you will see in these pages, a growing number of the world's brightest scientists are now actually coming out in favour of reincarnation. They say it is a viable way to explain certain fundamental features of our reality and consciousness. Scientists – medical doctors, biologists, physicists and neurologists – are taking a second look at reincarnation simply because that's where the science is leading them.

These are exciting times.

Just a few decades ago, a book like this one could not have been written. Even the height of the burgeoning 1960s New Age movement could not have anticipated the amazing breakthroughs in biology, neuroscience and quantum mechanics that are happening today - and what these mean to the concept that after we die, we can come back to life again.

Bentreshyt – A Priestess of Isis

The New York Times called the story of Irish born Dorothy Eady:
One of the Western World's most intriguing and convincing modern case histories of reincarnation.
For most of her long life, Eady came to be known as Omm Sety, which means Mother of Seti. This is because she named her son Seti, and Omm is the Egyptian word for mother.
Seti was a powerful Egyptian pharaoh who lived around 1300 B.C. He was the father of one of the most well-known Egyptian rulers, Ramesses II. Also known as Ramesses the Great, he is the pharaoh sometimes purported to be the pharaoh of the Bible's Book of Exodus. It was Ramesses II who refused the demands of Moses to free the Hebrew people from slavery, only to face the devastating wrath of God. The role of Ramesses II in the story of Moses has never been verified by historians or archaeologists, however, and is hotly disputed by many others. This is also fiercely contested by Omm Sety herself, as we shall see, because she knew him personally.

Early Life
However, before we get too far ahead of our story, let's go back to the beginning of the remarkable journey of Omm Sety, born as Dorothy Eady in 1904 in London. Her parents, Reuben and Caroline Eady, were Irish and had come to England to find better economic opportunities.
Raised in a small English coastal village, little Dorothy

Eady was a normal child until the age of three when she took a tumble down a stairway. She landed on her head and sustained a major injury. Unfortunately her condition was so serious that doctors told her parents to prepare themselves for the worst and, in fact, pronounced her dead at one point.

But Dorothy clung to life, and somehow survived. Doctors were stunned by this turn around and called her recovery a miracle.

However, when Dorothy awoke from her coma she was a changed person. Her behaviour was described, with typical British reserve, as 'strange'.

But even more bizarre was that this three year old girl now seemed to have developed an intense interest in all things Egyptian. Little Dorothy began to speak of the ancient Egyptian religion and even of obscure, forgotten or unknown rituals and customs. How she had come to gain this kind of knowledge was a profound mystery.

Her personality was also different. It was almost as if there was another person inside her, sharing the same body. Dorothy was still Dorothy, but there was the tantalizing feeling that 'someone else' was there too and that this 'other' personality had merged with the Dorothy personality.

Whatever the case, her sudden alarming knowledge and love of ancient Egyptian culture got her kicked out of her Sunday school classes. Her teacher said that Dorothy began comparing Christianity unfavourably to the pagan deities of the faraway lands of the Nile. Although her teachers and parents were scandalized by this turn of events, they were also left feeling profoundly perplexed by the situation.

A major turning point came when Dorothy's parents

brought her to the British Museum on a family outing one day. Here she encountered a series of photographs showing sites of ancient Egypt's New Kingdom, an era identified by historians as extending from about 1550 B.C. to 1070 B.C. Upon seeing the photos, little Dorothy became energized and animated. She cried out:

"This is my home! But where are the trees? Where are the gardens?"

She proceeded to run through the rest of the museum excitedly, sometimes stopping to kiss the feet of statues and shouting out her joy to be amongst her people.

Dorothy's dumbfounded parents coped as well as they could. They struggled to come to terms with the strange behaviour of their daughter, and perhaps compensated by coming to an acceptance that she had somehow developed a natural, although unusually intense, interest in Egyptology.

Dorothy went on to shape her schooling around the study of ancient Egypt, including learning the language and reading and writing hieroglyphics.

Her absorption into Egyptology also took a number of paranormal turns. At the age of fifteen, Eady claimed to have been visited by 'the mummy' of Pharaoh Seti I. She also developed a tendency to sleepwalk and spontaneously entered into a trancelike state, during which she seemed to be communicating with unseen beings who spoke an ancient form of Egyptian.

She also reported out-of-body experiences and the 'transportation of her consciousness to strange realms'. This behaviour resulted in commitment to a sanitarium on a number of occasions.

After Eady grew to womanhood her great knowledge of Egypt helped her get a job writing articles and creating cartoon illustrations for an Egyptian public relations magazine which was produced in London. Through a connection at work, she met and married an Egyptian man living and studying in England. Her new husband was an English teacher and when he was offered a job back in his native country, he and his British bride returned to Egypt.

On the day Dorothy arrived in Egypt, she immediately dropped to her knees, fell to the ground and kissed the soil. She said:

"I'm finally home, and I'm never leaving again."

She would keep that promise over the next fifty years until the end of her life. Two years after arriving in Egypt, her husband was offered a much higher paying job in Iraq which would mean that Omm Sety would have to leave Egypt to continue her married life with her husband. But rather than leave, she filed for divorce. She was staying put.

Before her marriage broke down, Dorothy gave birth to a son whom she named after her 'spiritual mentor' Seti I, and thus came to be known as Omm Sety, Mother of Seti.

Visitations by Ho-Ra

Sometime during her early years in Egypt, Omm Sety began receiving visitations from an ancient Egyptian spirit figure that identified itself as Ho-Ra. Over a period of twelve months, Ho-Ra visited Dorothy (now known as Omm Sety) a number of times and dictated to her the details of a previous life he said she had lived in ancient Egypt.

Ho-Ra told her that her name had been Bentreshyt, which means 'Harp of Joy'. Her parents in her previous life were of humble means as her mother was a vegetable seller and her father, a blonde haired blue eyed man of Greek descent, was a soldier in the army of Seti I. The mother of Bentreshyt died when she was three and because her father was away at war and also could not afford to support a child, Bentreshyt was brought to a religious temple where she was raised to be a priestess of Isis.

As a priestess of Isis, Bentreshyt was to live her life as a consecrated virgin, taking her vows at the age of twelve. She would play an important role in rituals related to the annual celebration of the passion and resurrection of Osiris, the god of the underworld and husband of Isis.

Ho-Ra told Omm Sety that Bentreshyt lived to the age of fourteen, and died under tragic circumstances by taking her own life. Her end was the direct result of a chance meeting with the Pharaoh himself, Seti I. It seemed that Seti had visited the temple of Isis on one occasion and in a garden had spotted the young priestess, Bentreshyt, who was just thirteen or fourteen years old. He instantly became infatuated with the beautiful young girl, particularly because she had inherited the blonde hair and stunning blue eyes of her Greek father, setting her apart from the standard dark hair and eyes of the average Egyptian female of the day.

Seti took her as his lover and she became pregnant.

Because a priestess of Isis was expected to remain virginal for life, and because her pregnancy was the result of a dalliance with the Pharaoh himself, the resulting scandal would have been enormous. Bentreshyt only admitted to being pregnant and naming the father after being tortured. Once admitting her guilt, she was still to face trial - but it was a foregone conclusion that she would be found guilty based on her own confession.

The penalty, she knew, would be death. Thus, rather than face it all, Bentreshyt killed herself.

Life as Omm Sety
After an intensive year channelling the spirit of Ho-Ra, Omm Sety came to fully understand and accept herself for who and what she really was - the reincarnation of an ancient priestess of Isis who had lived and died under tragic circumstances some three thousand years ago.

The knowledge she had gained through her remarkable paranormal experience, combined with her formal education, meant that Omm Sety commanded skills and knowledge that would serve her well in Egypt. She was equipped like practically none other to play a key role in assisting the many scholars and archaeologists who were swarming all over Egypt at the time, uncovering the secrets of the ancient kingdoms.

Her unique knowledge was extremely fortunate in terms of allowing her a way to support herself and her son financially, and without a husband. Most of the early to mid-20th Century was a time when women were second-class citizens and expected to stay home, have children, be mothers and keep the home fires burning. For a woman to work and hold an important position was frowned upon. It was the men who were expected to earn a living for their families.

This was especially true in Egypt where there was even stronger cultural pressures for women to maintain their place in society as a secondary adjunct to men.

Uncommon Knowledge
After she divorced her husband, Omm Sety moved to Nazlat as Samman, situated near the Giza pyramids,

where she met Selim Hassan, the archaeologist who would one day write an amazing sixteen volume Encyclopedia of Ancient Egypt. Accomplishing this monumental task probably would have been far more difficult if it had not been for the uncanny, unnatural knowledge and strong writing skills of Omm Sety.

She worked for Hassan as his secretary and draughtswoman. In this position she was able to meet and interact with dozens of other scientists, historians, archaeologists and Egyptologists who were uncovering the secrets of the pharaohs. She became a well-known figure and her amazing skills, combined with an unparalleled knowledge of where major archaeological finds might be uncovered, contributed to her legend.

For example, after the discovery of the Temple of Seti I in Abydos, Omm Sety said that she remembered a garden area that was a part of the temple complex. Few believed that a garden would have been included in such a temple, but Omm Sety told them exactly where to dig, and it would be found. It was. Omm Sety said she remembered spending time in the garden during her life as Bentreshyt.

Omm Sety described entering the Temple of Seti as being like accessing a time machine. When she was inside, she said it was as if the past and present 'combined as one' and she was able to compare the vastly different outlooks and mindset of the ancient people as opposed to modern people of her era. She said that the modern mind had extreme difficulty in comprehending a world in which magic was the norm. She also said that the magic really worked.

She explained that scenes depicted on temple walls could 'be activated' by the mind of ancient Egyptians to produce real world results.

As for Ramesses the Great, Omm Sety considered him to be the most slandered pharaoh of her time. As we said earlier, Ramesses II is often tagged with being the wicked pharaoh who defied the God of Moses, who ordered the death of all first-born sons in his kingdom, and who kept the Hebrew people in a state of cruel slavery.

But Omm Sety claims to have personally known and met Ramesses II in her previous life as Bentreshyt. At the time, Ramesses was a teenage boy, who went on to become a kind and just ruler upon the death of his father, Seti I. She said the connection of Ramesses II with the actions depicted in the Book of Exodus had nothing to do with him, and that his reputation had been falsely maligned by history. She also clearly remembered Ramesses as a teenage boy who was energetic, noisy, curious and intelligent.

Ramesses went on to become perhaps the greatest of New Kingdom pharaohs. Scholars agree he lived to an amazing age of ninety or ninety-one years old, that he was a brilliant military leader, and also created a climate of economic prosperity and security for his subjects at home in Egypt.

Lasting Legacy

Omm Sety stayed true to her word and never left Egypt. She died at the age of seventy-seven in Abydos. Throughout her life in Egypt she never attempted to hide her belief that she was the reincarnation of an Isis priestess of some three thousand years before - in fact she spoke of it openly, and didn't care whether people believed her or not. It helped that she was able to back up her claims time after time with astounding revelations about ancient Egyptian culture and religion that had been long forgotten, or completely unknown.

Many times a particular description of a ritual or custom as described only by Omm Sety would be verified with the discovery of a previously unknown manuscript found buried in some tomb or lost for centuries in the dusty halls of a museum warehouse.

Omm Sety not only claimed to be the reincarnation of an ancient priestess but was known to keep up the practices of the ancient religions. She brought offerings to the Temple of Seti and continued to perform rituals associated with the worship of Osiris. She was also known to practice ancient healing techniques used by the ancient Egyptians both on herself and others - and was credited with many amazing cures of chronic conditions.

Much of the knowledge that can be found today in textbooks and popular literature about the religions, culture and practices of ancient Egypt may have never been uncovered without the remarkable insights of Omm Sety. There are dozens of scholarly works - books, papers and reference materials, such as encyclopedias, that pay tribute to and acknowledge the deft assistance of Omm Sety as writer, interpreter, draughtswoman and researcher.

What modern science cannot acknowledge is the fact that a huge portion of the information she provided was the result of taking out-of-body trips to ancient Egypt itself, meetings with strange gods and wise beings, and her own personal memories of the life she lived three thousand years ago as a priestess of Isis.

The long life of Dorothy Eady, a little Irish-English girl who came to be known as one of the greatest

Egyptologists of the 20th Century, remains one of the most stunning and rock-solid cases for the validity of reincarnation. From the age of three until her death at the age of seventy-seven, she never recanted her claim to be the reincarnation of a fourteen year old priestess of Isis who lived in Egypt's New Kingdom some three thousand years before.

Her claims were backed up by decades of knowledgeable revelations about the life, times and customs of ancient Egypt, much of which was eventually proven to be true by the diggings of archaeologists and the study of historians.

If there ever was a case to prove the validity of the theory that people transcend death and can live again in a new body in a different era of time, it is the life of Dorothy Eady - Omm Sety.

The Reawakening of Marty Martin

Marty Martyn seemed to 'have it all' until a massive heart attack killed him in 1964.

Martyn lived the classic lifestyle of the rich and famous in Hollywood, California. He enjoyed all the trappings of the most successful movie stars. He owned a fabulous mansion with a large swimming pool in an exclusive Beverly Hills neighbourhood. He drove a Rolls Royse – well, we should say, his chauffeur drove the Rolls Royce for him.

He was surrounded in beautiful women and although he had been married and divorced four times, this hardly mattered to him as there was always another beautiful starlet on hand to attend to his needs. All of his friends were A-list movie stars or powerful studio executives. He also had influential friends outside the movie business, including high-ranking politicians from Washington D.C. They were eager to be his friend, or at least get friendly with his cash.

Marty Martyn was a classic rags-to-riches American success story. Born Morris Kolinsky in Philadelphia, he was the son of humble immigrants from the Ukraine. His father owned a small clothes press and tailor shop. As a young man Morris, along with his sister, decided to relocate to New York. He changed his name to Marty Martyn and got a job as a dancer in a Broadway play. His sister also successfully acquired theatre roles in dance and, after a short while, the brother and sister team made their way to Hollywood where they tried to break into the film industry.

Marty Martyn was able to land just one film role, a bit

part in the 1932 film Night After Night starring the then popular gangster turned movie star, George Raft. That small role turned out to be the peak of his acting career.

The connections he made whilst trying to make it as an actor eventually enabled him to open the Marty Martyn Talent Agency. Success and boat loads of cash soon followed. One of his early clients was Glenn Ford, who would go on to be a major Hollywood star.

Marty was also clever in his marriages, especially his fourth. He married the niece of Spyros P Skouras, who was the president of 20th Century Fox Studios. His new wife and her family were unimaginably wealthy. Marty's fourth wife owned one of the most palatial mansions in Hollywood - and this is where Marty was living when his luck finally ran out.

Morris Kolinsky, better known as Marty Marytn, contracted leukemia. But before this disease could take him, a major heart attack ended his life suddenly in 1964 at the age of sixty-one years old.

Did Marty Reawaken in a Small Oklahoma Town?
But perhaps Marty Martyn is not so dead after all.

Recently a number of American newspapers began running the story of a five year old boy named Ryan who lives with his mother and father in a rural area of Muskogee County, Oklahoma.

Ryan began to experience terrible nightmares which caused him to wake up screaming:

"My heart is exploding!" and,

"Help me! I can't breathe!"

He would jump from his bed, white with terror and suffer numerous episodes of breathing difficulties and chest pains.

At the onset of the nightmares, little Ryan also began to speak of strange things - of people and places he should have no knowledge of. His parents first interpreted all this as gibberish. But the child was insistent about whatever he was talking about, and some of the things he had to say started to form a coherent story.

Ryan began to speak of 'the person who I really am'. He said this man had a much better and more interesting life than he. He said this person lived in a house with a swimming pool on Rocks Drive. He frequently mentioned missing one of his best friends who was 'very powerful' - this was a man he identified mysteriously as Senator Five.

Ryan eventually began to remember more. He started to talk about incidents of a life he once seemed to have lived in Hollywood and how glamorous, fun and interesting it was. He said that he had famous friends and knew a lot of beautiful women. He said he enjoyed dancing, wearing fancy clothes and going to the best restaurants - he especially liked Chinese food.

He then began to remember even more astonishing details. For example, he said he was a personal friend of the legendary movie star Rita Hayworth. He also knew Mae West. Little Ryan also said he had a sister who was a famous dancer, and that he had a daughter whom he dearly missed.

He told of trips to Paris and spending a lot of time on a 'big boat' in the Mediterranean off the shores of France and Italy. On one of these trips he got a terrible sunburn. Imagine a five-year-old boy commenting:

"If you want to see the world, there's no better way than to do it on a boat."

He talked often of a favourite café in the streets of Paris, and also the fabulous nightclubs of that city.

Ryan's stories contained tantalizing detail. For example, one time he said he was 'punched out' by the bodyguards of Marilyn Monroe just for trying to talk to her. Whenever Ryan would see an image of the famous white letters of the Hollywood sign on television, he would cry out:

"That's my home!"

Ryan began to urge his parents to 'find him'. His parents were completely dumbfounded by the strange behaviour of their son. They are small-town conservative, Bible-believing Baptists. His father, Kevin, is a police officer with thirteen years of experience, and his mother, Cyndi, works as a clerk for the county.

Kevin and Cyndi knew next to nothing about reincarnation and as conservative Christians, completely rejected the notion. It was antithetical to their strict Bible beliefs. But Ryan was so persistent in his claims of having lived a previous life in Hollywood, his mother began to document some of the specifics of what he was talking about. She eventually formed a list of one hundred and two items that might be checked against actual historical records.

The trouble was, Ryan could not recall what his name was in his supposed former life. He didn't think he was a famous movie star with a well-known name. If he was a significant figure in Hollywood, he must have been someone more obscure or who worked behind the scenes, yet well-connected in the movie and entertainment industry.

Cyndi went to the local library and brought home dozens of books about Hollywood, especially old Hollywood. One day, flipping through pictures taken from old black and white films, Ryan grew excited when he saw a picture of an actor standing next to the famous Hollywood star, George Raft.

"That's me, mama!" Ryan shouted out. "That's me and that's George. Mama, you found me!"

The picture of the actor standing next to George Raft was, of course, Marty Martyn, in a scene from the movie Night After Night – the only movie Martyn ever had a role in, and that was merely a 'bit' role. One of Ryan's specific memories was of a movie that had a 'closet full of guns'. Cyndi found out more details concerning Night After Night, and discovered that it included a scene wherein gangsters had collected a stash of guns kept in a closet.

Kevin and Cyndi then rented the movie Night After Night. Watching it was enough to convince them that whatever Ryan was talking about, there had to be something to it. Without seeing the film Ryan had described the plot of Night After Night in almost perfect detail. There was no chance that the little boy had ever seen the movie on TV - it was an obscure film that came and went from the theatre scene in just a few months back in 1932.

There was still a big problem, however. Because Marty Martyn's role was such a small part, he was not credited in the film. His small scene was even edited out in some releases of the film. His name did not appear in the credits rolling at the end of the movie, nor in any of the film's documentation.

Searching through a lot of photos, the closest they could come to finding a guy who looked like Marty was an actor by the name of Ralf Harolde - but this name did not ring a bell with Ryan.

Despite everything, Ryan's parents still refused to accept the possibility that their son was the reincarnation of a dead Hollywood movie star. On the other hand, they had learned that when children develop such reincarnation-like fixations, one of the best therapies for ridding them of their nightmares and anxieties is to learn as much as they can about the past life they seem to remember.

Ryan's memories were more than a curiosity. The child was obviously deeply troubled by his memories as he continued to suffer frequent nightmares and an agonizing feeling of loneliness and alienation. He said he found his current life as a boy in Oklahoma boring and that he wanted to go back to his house with the pool, dancing with pretty ladies and boating around the world.

His parents contacted Dr Jim Tucker, Medical Director of The Child and Family Psychiatry Clinic and Associate Professor of Psychiatry and Neurobehavioral Sciences at the University of Virginia.

Dr Tucker said that the best way to help Ryan was to assist him with identifying with the past-life personality in question. He said this might actually resolve the fixation Ryan had developed, whether his past-life memories were real, or some kind of delusion.

To this end, Kevin and Cyndi flew their son to southern California for a personal visit to Tinsel Town, still thinking that the actor they were looking for might be Ralf Harolde. Through careful research, they were able to find the neighbourhood and likely locations where Harolde lived during his life, but nothing seemed familiar to Ryan.

There were also other problems associated with Ralf Harolde. Ryan said that in his previous life he had a sister who was a famous dancer but Ralf Harolde had no

sister. Other details of his life did not match up as well.
Still desperate to find answers for their son, Ryan's parents then hired a woman by the name of Kate Coe who was a professional film footage researcher. She searched through old Hollywood documents to find every scrap of information she could about the movie Night After Night and eventually she found the mysterious man who had just a brief cameo in the movie. He was finally identified – it was Marty Martyn, who went on to become a successful Hollywood talent agent.
Kate Coe was also able to collect numerous photos of Marty Martyn at various stages of his life. Ryan's parents and Dr Tucker used the photographs to formulate a test for the boy. They gathered the pictures of numerous other people, including old film stars, and placed photos of Martyn among groups of other photographs. They asked Ryan to point out which picture was the man he claimed to be in his previous life.
Ryan pointed to the correct photo one hundred percent of the time. He was able on all occasions to point to Marty Martyn among groups of diverse photograph collections.
Dr Tucker also took the one hundred and two points of Ryan's past-life incidents documented by Ryan's mother and was able to verify ninety-two of them as being accurate events that coincided with the life of Marty Martyn. Ryan was even able to correctly identify a picture of Martyn's former wife, and of his daughter.
After this research was complete, Dr Tucker suggested that Kevin and Cyndi bring their young son to Hollywood one more time as the doctor had arranged a meeting between Ryan and the woman he had identified as the daughter of Marty Martyn. Martyn's daughter agreed to meet the child – even though she was now the

same age as Ryan's grandmother.

When Ryan and the woman met, Ryan felt deep sadness and surprise at how old his daughter had become. He said:

"I feel so bad, she got so old. Why didn't she wait for me?"

Martyn's daughter asked Ryan a barrage of questions about her father and life, including incidents that were private family moments that only the real Marty Martyn could have known - and Ryan was able to answer just about every question correctly.

They were even able to uncover who the mysterious Senator Five Ryan spoke of as being one of his best friends. It turned out that Marty Martyn was good friends with a U.S. Senator from New York whose name was Senator Irving Ives. It also transpired that Marty's last place of residence - the one with the big swimming pool which Ryan said was on Rocks Drive - was located at 825 N. Roxbury.

Fortunately for the long-distressed parents of little Ryan, his meeting with the daughter of the man whom he thought he previously was and learning about his life, had the effect of easing his anxiety and quelling his nightmares. The in-depth investigation of the life of the former Hollywood talent agent seemed to bring a measure of peace and resolution to the young child. His memories of his past life began to fade into the background, and he began to more fully embrace who he was today - an ordinary boy in a small Oklahoma town.

To this day, Kevin and Cyndi say the incidents with their son have not brought them over to a belief in reincarnation. Even Dr Jim Tucker is hesitant to label the case as one that provides actual proof that people die and come back again as new individuals living in a different time and place. All he will admit is that time and time again, when such cases come up, the treatment for allying the anxieties of children with apparent past-life memories is to confront those memories directly, which enables them to forget and move on.

Yet the facts of the case speak for themselves. Is there any other logical explanation for how Ryan could remember so many details of the life of a now obscure and all but forgotten Hollywood talent agent? If this is not a case of actual reincarnation, then what is it?

Past Lives on Other Planets

Many people today still find the idea of reincarnation as a 'way out there' concept. If they consider the idea at all, they relegate the suggestion of past lives to either wacky New Agers or those who subscribe to eastern religions, such as Hinduism or Buddhism.

On the other hand, belief in reincarnation has been gaining steady acceptance among the general European and American populations, with some surveys showing that as many as twenty-five percent of people in Western industrialized nations now believe in reincarnation.

But just when you think things can't get any stranger, they often do.

Perhaps it was only a matter of time before the world of reincarnation and the highly strange realm of UFOs and alien abduction phenomenon collided.

Today dozens of people have come forward to make the claim that not only are they reincarnated but in their previous existence they were an alien from another planet, or possibly another dimension in time or space. They also claim that extraterrestrials are deeply involved in a kind of long-term process of engineering the human race - and reincarnation is the 'engine which drives that process'.

Some UFO researchers says that ETs are directing the evolution of the human species toward certain specific goals, a large part of the process involving the manipulation of how people, or their souls, reincarnate.

One person who said she has had direct experience with 'alien manipulation of souls' is Suzanne Hansen of New Zealand. Hansen just also happens to be director of

UFOCUS NZ, which is the largest UFO research group in New Zealand.

In a television interview with a New Zealand news team, Suzanne Hansen told reporters that when she was an eight year old child she was abducted and taken aboard an ET spacecraft where she met a crew of the classic 'grey aliens'. On board the ship, the greys introduced her to a 'ball of light' which Hansen sensed was more than a mere energy orb, but possessed a kind of intelligence - as if it were a free floating 'soul'.

The aliens then had something astonishing to tell her: They said that many years later she would marry and become pregnant with the fetus of a male child. At some point, the aliens said they would return to 'insert' the ball of light Suzanne encountered as a child into her fetus, and that this ball of light was a specially engineered 'soul' which would shape the life and consciousness of her future son.

Years later, Hansen married and became pregnant with a male child, and the 'soul insertion' procedure was carried out by the ETs, as promised.

All of these events were recalled via the process of hypnotic regression, in this case carried out by one of the world's leading proponents of such work – Mary Rodwell, an Australian who began her career as a nurse, and transitioned to becoming a highly respected psychological therapist who specializes in helping people who say they have been traumatized by an alien abduction experience. Rodwell has conducted thousands of such sessions with patients from all over the world.

With Mary Rodwell's help, Suzanne recalled being told by the ETs that her son would embody a special set of abilities, including greater psychic capabilities, powers of healing and an aptitude to work with exotic levels of inter-dimensional energies, as well as being able to communicate with non-human beings. The child would also become involved with certain 'greater projects' such as healing the planet and raising the consciousness of other human beings in terms of developing more harmonious ways to live within the ecosystem of the earth.

Hansen said that the ETs explained that her son would have no conscious memory of any of these abilities, but that he would begin to become more aware of his custom-engineered talents when he reached the age of about thirty-five years old.

Suzanne Hansen describes herself as a 'lifetime abductee'. She believes that extraterrestrials have been visiting her, taking her aboard their crafts, and working with her throughout her life. She has come to accept that the ETs are benign and working for the betterment of the human species, including their work to imbue a specific population of people with advanced abilities - all directed toward 'improving the species' and rescuing the planet which is on a dangerous path of war, over-population and widespread ecological destruction.

Other Lives - Other Planets

But reincarnation from lives on other planets does not necessarily need an ET-UFO connection. Long before researchers in the ufology community began considering the reincarnation process as part of the abduction experience, some of the more recent pioneers in past-life regression therapy have been finding instances of people who claim to recall past lives that originate on far-off planets or alien worlds.

One of the most well-known and respected advocates of past-life regression therapy is Dr Michael Newton, a counselling psychologist who has performed thousands of hypnotic sessions in which he has regressed patients to memories of past lives.

Dr Newton's ground-breaking 1994 book, Journey of Souls, found a large public audience and helped both popularize and legitimize the idea of not only life after death and reincarnation, but the situation of life-between-life - that is, the activities of the soul in the time after a person dies, but before the person decides to reincarnate again physically into a new life and time.

Early on in his practice, Dr Newton was initially surprised when some of his patients would spontaneously begin speaking of past life scenarios. At the time, Newton was an avowed atheist. He has stated bluntly that in his early career he would have never considered past-life regression therapy to be something that would be even remotely legitimate. But it was the spontaneous reports of his own patients that changed his mind.

Memories of past lives would surface during a hypnotic session in which Newton was attempting to guide a patient back to early childhood, hoping to uncover some trauma that was causing the person trouble in his or her current adult life. But instead of stopping at say the age of one year or six months, many people would just 'keep going' until they found themselves living in a previous century with a different name, body and identity.

Although highly resistant to the idea at first, Dr Newton also could not help but notice that once a person revisited a past life, the problems in their current life would be alleviated. For example, if a person reports a past life in which he or she drowned, they may have an inexplicable phobia about water in their current life. By reliving the past-life incident of drowning, the present-life fear of water vanishes for the patient.

Once Dr Newton became more familiar and comfortable with past-life regression therapy, he also began to notice that some people would report the experience of being 'a soul' or perhaps spirit that was in between reincarnations. It would seem that there is a certain period of time where a person/soul has time to pause, rest and evaluate their experience in the life they have just completed before entering into a new life.

But a certain percentage of hypnotically regressed people had something more bizarre to report - that of being an intelligent life form living on another planet. One of the most common of these kinds of reports were people who claimed to live as underwater beings in an ocean environment - sometimes on a planet which was composed entirely of water, or with just a single tiny continent.

In other instances, Newton had people tell him that they recalled being an intelligent winged being living in an exotic forest environment on a strange planet.

In a television interview, Dr. Newton said:

"What is interesting in talking to people who have incarnated on other worlds is that there is a similarity here ... it may be that people who come here also like to go to other worlds because what appeals to them about earth appeals to them about another environment that is somewhat similar.

"For instance, when I'm talking to large audiences I ask how many people have had dreams where they could fly. Usually seventy-five percent of them will raise their hands. Then I will say how many of you have had dreams where you could swim under water and breathe, and that you are a very intelligent life form. About half will do that. Then I really narrow the field down, I will ask, how many have been giants in their dreams … only a few hands … and then I ask how many have been really tiny beings where everything else is larger than you are, and just one or two out of a group of one hundred or two hundred people will raise their hands.

"And what this indicates is that … many people who incarnate on earth also incarnate on flying or water worlds. And so I have had a number of clients who have talked to me about being flying creatures, highly intelligent flying creatures on other worlds and what those worlds were like, and the same for water and how they can swim deep into an ocean kind of atmosphere, how there are cities under the ocean, and they look like not whales or dolphins so much … but creatures that are so strange that we see them only in mythology … I think a lot of our mythologies may well come from our early memories …"

Some incarnation on other worlds would seem to almost defy any familiar description. For example Dr Newton states:

"In one case, a man is regressed to another planet where he began his incarnations on a dark, quiet world with intelligent, although unemotional, life forms who were dying as a race. This was a world devoted to reason and logic. Eventually, (he) asked for a transfer to a brighter world where he could incarnate into a more sensitive being. He was given Earth."

Michael Newton is not the only hypnotherapist who has encountered subjects who claim to be reincarnated from strange life forms on other planets. Another is professional hypnotherapist Dolores Cannon who has authored seventeen books (to date) cataloguing the thousands of subjects she has regressed over a remarkable fifty years of hypnosis practice.

Among the past life incarnations Cannon's subjects have reported are:

*A woman who said her previous life was that of an energy sun being.

*A man who was an intelligent robot with 'real consciousness' in a far off planet.

*A man who lived as a Bigfoot or Sasquatch-like creature.

*Souls who have never incarnated on earth before.

*Other dimensional beings.

*Citizens of lost civilizations such as Atlantis and Lemuria.

What cases like these show is how the idea of reincarnation is not only gaining more acceptance today among a modern audience, including a population that is not necessarily religious, but that the very nature of reincarnation itself is also evolving to a more complex form, and rapidly.

Part of the reason is that people today are naturally applying the findings of modern science and quantum mechanics theory to the ancient concept of reincarnation. Just a few decades ago, for example, most people would have naturally assumed a linear time progression for incarnational lives - a person who died in 1885, for example, could only be born again in some year after that time, say, 1910.

The assumption was that a 'soul' began its reincarnation journey in ancient times, perhaps even the Stone Age, and progressed century-by-century to the modern times.

But after the work of Albert Einstein and others showed that time is a 'relative' quantity or phenomenon, that time is fluid, can flow backwards and forwards, and is not linear at all - well, the implications for reincarnation become obvious as well.

Beyond that, quantum theory has also opened up our conception of the universe from being a singular kind of existence to that of a 'multiverse' - that our reality may actually be one of multiple dimensions, perhaps even infinite dimensions, and that 'souls' can cross over between dimensional time and space, backwards and forwards, sideways and other ways - creating a much more rich and complex dynamic of how reincarnation actually works.

Since just about everyone today believes that there is life on other planets, and most likely intelligent life, it is not a great leap to consider the possibility that human beings can incarnate as other beings living on other planets, and vice versa - and indeed, the evidence from actual hypnotic regression sessions seems to be showing that is exactly the case.

It seems that just when more people are becoming comfortable with the traditional and ancient concept of reincarnation, the game is about to change again, or we should say, the game is changing and evolving before our very eyes.

The Interesting Case of Sherrie Lea Laird and Marilyn

One of the biggest points of ridicule directed at people who claim to have been reincarnated is when they declare to be the rebirth of a famous or powerful person, such as an Egyptian queen, an American Civil War general, an ancient wise man, or perhaps a famous movie star.

Sceptics ask in sneering tones:

"Why don't people ever seem to be the reincarnation of some Average Joe, like some bored housewife, a bum or homeless man?"

Well the fact is the vast majority of people claiming to be reincarnated do not remember the past life of a famous person. The overwhelming majority of people who have undergone hypnotic regression describe utterly ordinary past lives - a lowly slave, a farm worker, a truck driver, a failed artist.

This is affirmed by the pioneers of past-life regression, such as Dr Michael Newton, Dr Brian Weiss, Dolores Cannon, Dr Ian Stevenson and many others. These researchers have collectively regressed thousands of people. They report that only a tiny fraction of patients - less than one-half of one percent - remember the past life of a famous or powerful person.

But sometimes it does occur.

Furthermore, when a person who happens to be already famous proclaims to be the reincarnation of some other famous person - well, that's a double whammy, and the sarcastic sceptics have an even greater field day.

Such is the case of a woman who gained a significant

amount of celebrity status when her Canadian pop band scored a flurry of charting hits in the late 1990s and early 2000s. The band was called Sulk. Its lovely blonde, talented and charismatic lead singer was Sherrie Lea Laird, a native of Edinburgh, Scotland, now living in Canada.

Laird began having visions and disturbing memories from around the age of nine years old. She felt as if there was another person inside of her. This 'inner person' was a powerful, artistic, yet deeply disturbed woman who seemed to be in a steady state of distress, unhappiness and sometimes morbid depression.

In most reincarnation cases, the memories of past lives fade as a person grows older and comes fully into their own personality. In the case of Sherrie Lea Laird, the opposite occurred. The inner woman that began troubling her as a little girl grew only louder and more controlling as the years passed. By the time she reached her mid-thirties, Laird was suicidal. In fact, she attempted suicide twice. The powerful woman who was haunting her in dreams, and also in waking memories, was making her life a living hell.

In desperation Laird sought the help of psychologists, but she found traditional therapies - talk therapy, Freudian-style psychoanalysis, antidepressant medications - all of little or no value.

Laird eventually learned of a unique doctor of psychiatry who was practicing in Los Angeles. His name was Dr Adrian Finkelstein. He was extremely accomplished and highly respected as a medical doctor and therapist, but he had also dared to go against the grain of his profession to embrace the controversial practice of hypnotic past-life regression therapy.

In October of 1998, Dr Finkelstein was contacted by Laird, who by this time was convinced she was being tormented by past life memories of none other than one of the most iconic movie stars of all time.

It seems that the powerful 'inner woman' that had been tormenting Laird all her life was none other than Marilyn Monroe.

Extraordinary Claim, Extraordinary Proof.
After many years of working with Laird, Dr Finkelstein concluded that Sherrie Lea was not delusional and that she was indeed the bone fide reincarnation of Marilyn Monroe.

He also emphasized that in his opinion this was conclusive beyond a reasonable doubt.

The case was so convincing that Dr Finkelstein wrote a best-selling book about it titled, Marilyn Monroe Returns: The Healing of a Soul.

His conclusion about Laird as Monroe is based not only on the astonishing amount of information garnered from Laird's past-life memories as Marilyn Monroe but is also backed up by something much more solid and measurable - biometric identifiers.

Biometric identifiers are distinctive measurable characteristics used to label and describe individuals. They are physiological characteristics related to the shape of the body. For example, fingerprints, palm veins, face recognition, DNA, palm print, hand geometry, iris recognition, retina and odour/scent are all biometric identifiers. Biometrics are used by computers that can scan faces and recognize them according to the measurement of facial features, such as nose width, eyebrow placement, chin size and shape, and more.

Governments are using this technology today in airports, for example, to track terrorists or criminals. Video cameras can scan thousands of faces every second, relay the information to a biometrics database, and the computer can make an almost instant assessment of a person and match them to existing photographs of suspects using the characteristics of their facial structure.

When the biometrics of the face of Marilyn Monroe were measured against the face of Sherrie Laird, there were so many exact matches it meant that there was less than an 0.001 percent chance that so many 'hits' could have occurred by accident. Even if Monroe and Laird had been actual biological twins the biometrics could not have been as close a match.

There is another class of biometrics which can be measured in addition to those mentioned above. These are behavioural characteristics related to the pattern of how people speak, act and move, rather than specific features of the physical body. Behavioural traits include, but are not limited to, factors such as typing rhythm, walking gait, voice modulation and more. Here again, Monroe and Laird were a remarkable match.

Biometric data combined with the fact that Sherrie Laird could recall historically verifiable facts about Marilyn Monroe - including details never revealed in books or articles - makes this case of reincarnation among the most rock solid ever documented.

Life Stories
Of course, we all know that Marilyn Monroe led one of the most sensational, glamorous and tragic lives of the 20th Century, including three marriages, two of them to other famous luminaries, baseball superstar Joe

DiMaggio and playwright Arthur Miller.

Among her most salacious and scandalous exploits was her not-so-secret sexual relationship with the President of the United States, John F Kennedy.

Under hypnosis, Laird recalled numerous sexual encounters with the President, beginning when he was still a U.S. Senator from Massachusetts. The affair engendered little in the way of love or comfort for the troubled blonde bombshell. Under hypnosis, and speaking as Marilyn, Laird described Kennedy as 'horrible'. Channelling Marilyn, Laird said she also had sex with the brother of the President, Bobby Kennedy, who was the U.S. Attorney General at the time. One of these sleazy liaisons took place in the back seat of a chauffeured limo.

Laird poured cold water on the numerous conspiracy theories that have persisted over the death of Marilyn Monroe. One such theory says she was murdered by the CIA or U.S. Secret Service to cover up her illicit relationship with the President and his brother. But none of these agencies had anything to do with her death Laird revealed under hypnosis. It was an accidental overdose of drugs and alcohol during a typical bout of severe depression.

She also quashed the long-standing rumour that she had a fling with Elvis Presley. "Never happened," Laird said to a BBC reporter who was invited to sit in on one of her regression sessions with Dr Finkelstein.

Under the guidance of Dr Finkelstein, Laird re-experienced her death as Monroe, which she described as an event proceeded by difficulty breathing and then a crushing pain in the chest. Monroe's official cause of death was an overdose of barbiturates combined with alcohol and a cocktail of other drugs. These medications would have worked by shutting down her cardio-pulmonary system, so this too supports Laird's account.

In fact, Sherrie Laird had been tormented with chest pains and difficulty breathing from the time she was fourteen years old. Doctors never found a medical cause for this trauma, and considered her condition psychosomatic - although nothing specific in the life of the young Sherrie Laird could be identified to have precipitated such a psychological effect.

After Dr Finkelstein helped Laird relive her perceived death as Marilyn, the chest pains and breathing problems were relieved, never to bother her again.

As Laird progressed through her therapy, numerous coincidental elements between the lives of Monroe and Laird were uncovered. For example, Sherrie was making her living as a singer and entertainer, and Marilyn was an actress and singer. In one of Monroe's movies, Bus Stop, she played a singer named Cherie. Both Monroe and Laird married and divorced a former military service man early in their lives. Both women had an Aunt Anne in their family history … these kind of coincidences, which Dr Finkelstein prefers to call 'synchronicities' were many.

Mother and Daughter Return Together

But there is an even more incredible twist to the Monroe-Laird story.

While Dr Finkelstein was treating Sherrie Laird, her daughter asked to be hypnotically regressed - and she promptly recalled a past life in which her name was Gladys Baker. Gladys Baker was the mother of Marilyn Monroe, whose birth name was Norma Jean Mortenson, but soon after changed to Norma Jean Baker.

Amazingly, Gladys Baker died on 11 March 1984 - and Kezia Laird, the daughter of Sherrie Laird, was born almost exactly nine months later.

This revelation would seem to explain the strange dynamic between mother and daughter. While Sherrie Lea Laird was struggling with her life difficulties, which included involvement in the typical drug and alcohol abuse associated with the fast life of a rock star, her daughter Kezia took on the role of doting mother. Everyone who knew the pair said that Kezia struggled to restrain her mother from the excesses of her lifestyle, offered comfort during her periods of deep depression, and handled countless domestic chores. Kezia even sought to ensure that her mother was eating properly.

Thousands of reincarnation case files show that two people or groups of people often agree to return together. Therapists note that a husband and wife will frequently return to a new life together - but just as often with the roles reversed. The husband will reincarnate as the wife and the wife as the husband.

It appears that Marilyn and her mother had a pact to come back and experience life together again, this time with roles reversed.

Outstanding Credibility and Direct Experience

Even the most caustic of critics find it difficult to dismiss Laird's belief that she is the reincarnation of Marilyn Monroe (although dozens of highly critical articles have been published). But what the sceptics tend to gloss over is that Dr Adrian Finkelstein is a consummate medical professional who has achieved levels of success that few others have attained in his field.

Finkelstein was born in Romania to a Jewish family. With his mother and father, he escaped the great suffering and cruel oppression of the political situation in his home country by immigrating to Israel. Here Finkelstein continued the study of medicine he had begun while in Romania, even though he spoke no Hebrew or English. His nimble mind picked up a working understanding of both languages in about six months.

After completing his residency in Israel, Finkelstein made his way to the United States to practice medicine and psychiatry at the Menninger School of Psychiatry in Topeka, Kansas, which is widely considered the best facility of its kind in the United States. His work there on dream therapy was honoured with prestigious awards by both the Menninger School and Central Neuropsychiatric Association. He was also the first recipient of the A E Bennett Award, one of the highest honours in psychiatry.

After leaving Menninger, Finkelstein became Director of the Outpatient Psychiatry Division of Mount Sinai Hospital in Chicago. He also served as Professor of Psychiatry at the Chicago Medical School's University of Health Sciences.

Before he became involved in past-life regression therapy, Finkelstein had earned a reputation as one of the preeminent psychiatric doctors in the United States, and the world - but it was a special experience that launched him into a realm that most of his peers simply could not accept as legitimate.

One day while deeply involved in preparing a research paper in his office, Dr Finkelstein suddenly and unexpectedly felt an odd feeling come over him and he fell into a spontaneous reverie. He felt as if he had entered that state of mind that we sometimes experience between sleeping and wakefulness - what sleep researchers call the hypnogogic state. While in this hinterland between sleep and wakefulness, Finkelstein began to see himself, or experience himself, as being a different person.

Much to his wonderment, he was now a woman!

Information flooded into his mind about the woman he had inexplicably come to embody within his trance state. He described her as being unattractive, unmarried and middle-aged but also that she was a competent doctor. He could easily perceive the country she lived in - it was Iran. Other details of her life became known to him. Her father was a carpenter, for example. He even perceived her name - Thelma Sangiavi.

Finkelstein found himself being carried through the life of the woman as if watching it all in a movie, although it was as if he was an actor in that movie, playing the main character. When he came to the end of her life, he relived her death, the result of cancer. After death she floated out of her body, and her spirit proceeded to enter an area of bright glowing light.

Finkelstein realized that the woman was himself in a previous life.

The vision ended as suddenly as it began. When he came back to his normal senses, he was left in a state of astonishment. The vision had been as real - even more real - as anything he had ever experienced in his life. There was no question in his mind about what the vision meant. He had a knowingness, a certainty that he had lived previously as a female doctor in Iran.

This experience prompted Dr Finkelstein to pursue a further series of past-life regressions. Under hypnosis, he was able to remember twenty-four past lives, eleven of which were male and thirteen female.

After completing this thorough self-examination of who he was and where he had been through centuries of time, Dr Finkelstein realized it was necessary to end his career as a practitioner with established medical institutions to enter private practice. He came to believe that past-life regression was an incredibly powerful tool that could be used to heal people who are here today, but suffering from mental anguishes anchored in the past. These kinds of psychological problems were highly resistant to mainstream therapies, but past-life regression yielded near miraculous results.

His distinguished accomplishment in medicine, combined with his personal experience in past-life regression, placed him in a unique position of understanding, and enabled him to become a healer quite unlike any other.

Thus, if Dr Adrian Finkelstein has concluded that Scottish-Canadian pop star Sherrie Lea Laird is the bona fide reincarnation of Marilyn Monroe … well, there's probably no better authority on the planet to make that claim, and for that claim to be true.

Life on Mars

Just when it seems that so many of us are becoming comfortable with the idea of reincarnation, a new twist to the phenomenon comes along that challenges our minds to stretch to a new level. In a previous chapter we got a taste of this when we discussed people who reported being reincarnated from other planets or other dimensions, or who may have come from various other forms of non-human beings in previous lives.

In this chapter we discuss some cases belonging to a special group of people who remember past-lives from one of our closest neighbours in the solar system - the planet Mars.

In the past century there have been many well documented examples of people who claim to have past-life memories when they not only lived on Mars, but embodied the lives of a highly advanced race of humanoid beings that once lived there, hundreds of thousands or possibly millions of years ago. They claim that these humanoids may be the ancestors of all people on earth today.

One of the first and most famous known case of a Martian reincarnation was a woman who called herself Hélène Smith, born in Geneva, Switzerland, in 1861. She died in 1929.

Her birth name was Catherine-Elise Müller. Her father was a fairly successful Hungarian merchant. Catherine led a normal life working in a commercial house until about the age of thirty when she became attracted to spiritualism and the occult.

The environment of the early 19th Century in Europe might be compared to the 1960s and 1970s in America and Great Britain when the New Age movement burst onto the scene, emerging from a generally more conservative, scientific era. In the late 19th Century and early 20th Century, people such as Madam Blavatsky were forming new modes of thought, such as Theosophy; others, such as C.W. Leadbeater and Annie Besant, were stirring up great interest in spiritualism – from astral travel and séances, to spirit channelling and meditation.

Hélène Smith embraced all the exciting new spiritualist activities and quickly discovered that she was a gifted medium and psychic, and also easily mastered the esoteric art of automatic writing. She had a natural ability to enter into deep trance states, during which she channelled an impressive variety of spirits and entities. She gained a considerable amount of fame by claiming the ability to channel the famous writer Victor Hugo, recording his words via automatic writing. Not only did she channel Hugo's after-death communications, but an analysis of Smith's automatic writing was a close match to that of the late great writer.

One of the spirits Smith frequently channelled was that of Alessandro Cagliostro, a famous occultist and notorious Italian adventurer who died in 1795. His real name was Giuseppe Balsamo, a scoundrel and professional conman who claimed to be the lover of Marie Antoinette. He is believed to have played a role in the famous Affair of the Diamond Necklace, a bold scheme to steal a set of priceless jewels from the French Crown.

As her reputation grew, Catherine-Elise Müller changed her name to Hélène Smith. She was clearly among the most gifted mediums of the day and continued to gain traction among Europe's high society.

Reincarnation and remembering past lives soon became a part of Smith's repertoire, but one of the many past lives she recalled was unlike any other spiritualist or occultist of her day.

Hélène Smith claimed to have lived a previous life on the planet Mars.

Not only could she recall vivid imagery of her former life on Mars, but she had enough sketching and painting talent to create intriguing pictures of the Martian landscape. She even channelled a unique Martian language and produced a strange hieroglyphic-like Martian alphabet.

All of this might be written off by sceptics as the wild imagination of a woman gifted with the talents of a science fiction writer, except much of her Mars work was conducted under the direction of one of the leading European psychologists of the day, Théodore Flournoy, a Professor of Psychology at the University of Geneva. Flournoy was a student of Freud himself, and also a close collaborator with the great Swiss psychologist Carl Jung.

Flournoy wrote a book about the amazing abilities of Hélène Smith titled From India to the Planet Mars published in 1899. It was an international best seller and it certainly helped Smith's reputation in that the book was taken seriously by the scientific-psychology community. Even Carl Jung was so impressed by the book he sought rights from the publisher to be its official German translator.

As the title suggests, Smith also claimed a previous life in ancient India, where she said she lived as Princess Simandini, eleventh wife of Prince Sivrouka Nayaka. This claim was bolstered by her incredible ability to speak an ancient version of the Sanskrit language. Some sceptics said she might have simply learned the language on her own, but the likelihood of this happening was impossibly remote. For one thing, the Sanskrit she spoke was an antiquated version which was significantly dissimilar to modern Sanskrit - which is what one would expect because all languages evolve considerably from their original forms over centuries of time.

Another of her incarnational lives is a bit more sensational - she claimed to have been Marie Antoinette, the ill-fated Queen of France who was executed in 1793. She learned this though her psychic connection with Giuseppe Balsamo. Of course, history says that Balsamo purportedly had an affair with the French Queen, and perhaps planned to rob her of a diamond necklace. It is known at least that he travelled within the circles surrounding the queen - thus, it seemed appropriate that Smith would make after-death contact with this man.

Incidentally, the spirit of Balsamo became an important intermediary for Smith as she channelled a variety of entities, including those who proclaimed to be Martians. In trance, Balsamo referred to himself as 'Leopold' and he became a significant gatekeeper through which much of the information was channelled through Hélène Smith.

But it was her tales of life on Mars that enthralled many. Her descriptions of Mars, its environment, flora, strange animals, Martian beings and landscape were complex and detailed. She said the Red Planet was populated by a race of humanoid beings that were roughly Asian in physiognomy. They got around Mars in both self-powered vehicles and aircraft. Smith described dog-like animals that had 'heads like cabbages' but which were highly intelligent. They were close companions to the

Martians, and could even take dictation if required.

Smith also described two distinct ages, or perhaps eras of Mars. The age of her original incarnation on the planet gave way to what she called 'Ultra-Mars'. This version of the Red Planet was populated by troll-like beings who bore little resemblance to humans. They were different from the more humanoid Martians in many ways, including the use of an ideographic language rather than a phonetic script.

Smith said that the Martian race was destroyed by some kind of catastrophic disruption in the planet's atmosphere, forcing a few survivors to make their way to earth to start over.

Smith's version of events is extremely interesting since many similar theories have recently been advanced today after the discovery of a number of curious structures on Mars, such as 'The Face on Mars', along with an array of objects that look like ancient pyramids.

Theories for an ancient, extinct civilization on Mars have also recently garnered support from an elite cadre of former U.S. Military spies who were trained as the world's first remote viewers. Remote viewing is a highly controlled and disciplined form of psychic ability developed by some of the top scientists in the world at California's prestigious Stanford Research Institute. U.S. Military Intelligence and the CIA used remote viewers to spy on the Soviet Union during the height of the Cold War, and the programme achieved an astonishing level of success.

Remote viewers were tasked to cast their minds to Mars and, to make a long story short, all of them confirmed that Mars was once inhabited by a highly advanced civilization of both human-like beings, and other advanced life forms. They also found via remote viewing methodology that Mars had suffered a catastrophic collapse of its atmosphere and environment, as Smith had already said, and that some of the Martian survivors escaped to Earth.

Keep all of this information in mind when considering our next incident of Mars reincarnation - this time a recent case reported in newspapers around the world about a small boy in Russia.

Russian Boy Claims Previous Life on Mars
This story of Mars reincarnation comes from a well-respected source, namely, Gennady Belimov, a Russian Professor of Engineering and Physics.

When not working on high technology projects for industrial clients, or teaching courses at the Volzhsky Institute of Humanities at the Volgograd State University, Belimov travels throughout Russia exploring what he calls anomalous zones - areas where paranormal activities seem more prevalent than others.

Belimov was told of a seven year old boy living in one such anomalous zone, in a remote area called the Medveditskaya Ridge which is north of Volgograd. The boy's name is Boriska, and his parents noticed something unusual about him almost from the day he was born.

When just fifteen days old he could hold up his head unsupported, and seemed totally aware of and curious about his environment. He started speaking his first words at the age of four months. By seven months he was speaking in complete sentences. His first sentence as a seven month old baby was:

"I want a nail."

He said these words while pointing to a nail poking out

of the wall. His parents were surprised that he even knew what a nail was. By the time he was one year and six months old, Boriska began to read the large type of newspaper headlines.

Professor Belimov was invited by the boy's family to meet the child because they wanted the professor's opinion on the strange stories Boriska had to tell - stories of having lived a previous life on the planet Mars.

Belimov tells of his first encounter with the boy:

"Imagine, when everyone was sitting around the bonfire in the evening, this little boy, about seven years old, suddenly and loudly demanded silence: he was going to tell us about the inhabitants of Mars and about their trips to Earth … someone was still chatting in a low voice, and then the boy strictly demanded our full attention, or else there would be no story."

Belimov described Boriska this way:

"… a round faced child with the big eyes, in a summer t-shirt and a cool baseball cap, completely unafraid of the adults … he began an unbelievable story. About the Martian civilization, about megalith-cities and Martian space ships, about flights to other planets, and about the country of Lemuria on Earth, about the life of which he knew personally, having at some point flown here from Mars to this huge continent in the middle of the ocean and had friends there…"

Boriska's mother is a doctor and dermatologist, and his father is a retired military officer. They said their little boy began to speak of outer space and cosmic topics when he was two years old. His parents confessed to being utterly perplexed about where he might have learned of such subjects, having never been exposed to astronomy, science fiction shows, not even any space cartoons or such movies as Star Wars.

Boriska expressed no fear at the thought of dying because he remembered clearly dying before, many times, only to experience his soul being reborn to enter an all new life, and into an all new era of time. Many of those previous lives were on Mars with his final Mars incarnation occurring when a planetary catastrophe was slowly destroying the Martian oceans and atmosphere.

Boriska said he came to earth more than eight hundred thousand years ago when there was an advanced civilization that many today call Lemuria, an Atlantis-type population that is said to have eventually disappeared from the earth under tragic circumstances, as did Atlantis. Boriska said he flew an interplanetary vessel to and from earth and conducted trade with the Lemurians, who he described as people who were giants, averaging some nine meters tall. He said it was also around eight hundred thousand years ago that the Lemuria was destroyed by some kind of massive continental disruption that was precipitated by super advanced technology gone wrong.

Boriska said life on Mars was dangerous and difficult. Not only was the natural environment deteriorating, but the planet was at war with a mysterious something he called 'the station' which he said that everyone fought against. There was a partial nuclear war and that, combined with natural calamities, all but wiped out most life on Mars.

Some Martians escaped to earth, but he said others remained behind and survived, and are still there today living miserable lives in bleak underground dwellings. The evil station he spoke of is still at least partially operational. Boriska said this facility is the agent that destroyed a number of recent Russian space probes sent to Mars.

Boriska was able to describe in detail one of the spacecraft used to travel between planets.

"We just launched and we were already near the Earth," he told Professor Belimov.

Boriska then used a piece of chalk to draw a triangular shaped spacecraft. He explained:

"There are six layers," he said. "The outer layer takes 25% of the durable material, the second layer takes 30% and is like rubber, the third takes another 30% and is again metal, 4% is a layer with magnetic properties … If you power the magnetic layer with energy, the apparatus can fly all over the universe…"

Boriska recalled not just a single past life on Mars, but many. He said he lived, died and reincarnated numerous times across a number of eras that perhaps spanned a million years, or more. He said that in the last hundreds of thousands of years, Mars struggled with serious water problems. That was because, due to natural causes which included a radical pole shift, Mars began to gradually lose its atmosphere and water. Boriska said that special ships were sent to Earth to get water and these were huge cylindrical crafts which also served as 'mother ships'.

Boriska said that the Martians developed an ambitious plan to alleviate the deterioration of the Martian environment by igniting a second sun in the solar system - they planned to do this by increasing the mass of the planet Jupiter to force its vast store of hydrogen gas to ignite into nuclear fission, and thus begin burning like a small sun. The project failed, however, when it was determined that not enough additional mass existed in the entire solar system to jump start Jupiter.

Boriska described the race of Martians he belonged to as being 'human like'. After seeing a picture of the classic 'grey aliens' he said:

"We didn't look like that. We were closer to the Atlanteans and Lemurians that used to live on earth."

Bioriska said he knew of the greys, but described them as not human and cruel and from another galaxy. Like Hélène Smith before him, Boriska also described a race of troll-like beings that maintained a presence on Mars. These beings he also described as not human.

Professor Belimov said that after the story of Boriska had leaked out to the press, his life has become difficult. Local people consider him to be a freak and unnatural. His superior intelligence is frightening to most adults and alienates him from children his own age. Boriska is a brilliant mathematician, reads at an advanced level and doesn't fit in at local schools and so cannot be placed with other students of his age group. At the same time, he is not welcome at university level - he has nowhere to go.

Belimov said Boriska's problems have been further compounded by his parents' recent divorce - he seems a child out of place, out of time, and perhaps even someone who stands outside his own race or species.

Professor Belimov said he is attempting to provide as much support to this remarkable child as he can under incredibly difficult cultural restraints. Belimov calls Boriska 'an Indigo child' which is a term many are using today to describe a new class of children who appear to have been born with advanced mental abilities. Some claim Indigo children began to appear worldwide in the 1980s and they may represent a new stage in the evolution of the human race. Others believe they may be the result of alien-human hybrid projects developed by UFO ETs.

Sceptics Say….
Of course, sceptics relegate all of this to the 'nonsense bin'. They point out that the planet Mars has long enthralled and captured the imagination of the human race. They cite the enormous popularity of books, such as The War of the Worlds by H.G. Wells and The Martian Chronicles by Ray Bradbury - and many others.

It has also been noted that even respected mainstream scientists have set off waves of Mars enthusiasm with well-intentioned, but false theories, about life on Mars. One of the most enduring was ignited when Italian astronomer Giovanni Schiaparelli announced that he had telescopically observed a system of canals on the Red Planet. However, Shiaparelli used the Italian word 'canali', which better translates to 'channel' describing a natural waterway. But to the English speaking world, 'canali' sounded more like 'canal' - and the implication was that a canal was something of artificial construction. The Italian astronomer probably did not mean to suggest that the 'canali' he observed were of artificial construction - but it was too late. The idea caught fire with the public imagination.

The impression that desperate Martians were heroically building canals to fight off natural disaster on Mars took hold, and even highly respected scientists such as Percival Lowell (the man who predicted the location of Pluto) became convinced that the canals were real, and being built by Martians. Sceptics say the Martian canal controversy demonstrates how easy it is for an erroneous idea to take hold in the public consciousness, especially when it comes to the planet Mars, and even among highly intelligent scientists.

It's not surprising then, sceptics say, that people who believe in reincarnation would adopt the idea that some of their previous lives were lived on our nearest neighbour in the solar system.

On the other hand, the details which come out of past-life memories of Mars are incredibly consistent across wide groups of people from all walks of life and different cultures. Just about everyone who claims a Mars past-life tells of the terrible ecological cataclysm that delivered a death blow to most life on the planet. Many also tell of the once close relationship between advanced Martians and highly advanced earth-bound civilizations, such as Atlantis and Lemuria.

That so many people who claim to be reincarnated Martians, and who also tell of a desperate fight to salvage its ravaged environment, may help to explain why observations such as Schiaparelli's 'canali' so easily gripped the public imagination - it may be that a genuine memory of such an actual event still haunts the subconscious minds of millions of people here on earth.

As we have seen, such reports have gained support from an entirely different front - that of remote viewing - but also from those who are taking a closer look at the imagery gathered from U.S. and Russian space probes. When some people look at satellite photos of Mars, they see pyramids, monuments and domes of artificial construction.

Theories abound. All are fascinating and ignite the imagination. The idea that people on earth are reincarnated Martians only adds to an already spicy and intriguing subject.

Group Reincarnation

On 22 December 1991, the normally business-as-usual Baltimore Sun published a remarkable feature story about a case of reincarnation. A paper such as the Baltimore Sun is not a likely venue for esoteric articles but, because this case was so unusual, the editors just probably couldn't pass it up, being as the subject was about group reincarnation.

It seems that dozens of residents of a small town in California had collectively uncovered past-life memories of living together in another small town in another century, and on the other side of the nation on the American East Coast, in Virginia.

It all started when a newspaper reporter working in the city of Lake Elsinore, a small community east of Los Angeles, sought the help of a hypnotherapist. The thirty-four year old woman was living in a state of persistent anxiety and stress. She was perplexed because the symptoms she was having had no apparent cause that she could think of in her daily life, or in recent memory. She had tried everything, from seeing psychologists and taking medications, to self-help books and meditation. Nothing seemed to work. So she thought she would give hypnotism a try.

The reporter, Maureen Williamson, contacted Dr Marge Rieder, a hypnotherapist accustomed to helping people stop smoking, lose weight or get rid of phobias. Dr Rieder found that Williamson was an excellent subject for hypnosis as she went under quickly and deeply. After sending Williamson deep into trance, Rieder was able to uncover a number of Maureen Williamson's repressed childhood memories, including one of being sexually molested at age five, in fact, on the day of her fifth birthday.

Dr Rieder was certain that uncovering and working through this traumatic childhood event would bring healing to Williamson, relieving her persistent feelings of anxiety and stress. To some extent, it did. But about a week later when Maureen Williamson was making some notes for a newspaper story she was working on, she suddenly wrote down a name: John Daniel Ashford.

It was as if her hand had scribbled the note by itself. It was like automatic writing.

Overtly, the name meant nothing to her, but she couldn't forget about it. It was just so odd the way it popped out of nowhere, the way her hand moved by itself. She had a nagging feeling about the name - an intuitive feeling that it meant something important. But it was a mystery. There was no one in her life she knew by the name of John Daniel Ashford.

She decided to explore the issue with her hypnotherapist. Back on Marge Rieder's couch, in deep trance, Maureen was instructed to reach out with her mind to the name of John Daniel Ashford. She immediately had the feeling that she was someone else - that her name was Rebecca Ashford, the wife of John Ashford - and that she had lived more than a hundred years ago in the era of the American Civil War, which was fought between 1861 and 1865.

She was also able to pinpoint that Rebecca and John had lived in the small town of Millboro, Virginia.

But that was only the beginning. As Dr Rieder encouraged Williamson to go further, she brought forth troubling details about the life of Rebecca Ashford. It seems she was a woman of loose morals, especially for the conservative times of the 1860s. She was a wife with children, but she had a number of sexual affairs with other men, including one with a dangerous man who was a Confederate army spy. When this affair was exposed, Sarah was raped and strangled as punishment. She remembered her death in gruesome detail, including the memory of 'blood coming out of her ears'.

It became clear that this horrible death and troubled past-life experience was a major contributor to the stress and anxiety for which she sought treatment. Uncovering these past-life traumas went even further towards helping Maureen find a sense of peace and balance.

But little did she know that her encounter with reincarnation was only just beginning.

As difficult as it was for Maureen Williamson to accept that she had lived before, she was in for another shock. That was because she would soon begin meeting the people she knew in her past-life as they were living along with her in her present-day community of Lake Elsinore.

The first person she recognized from her past-life was Joe Nazarowski, a man who worked as a security officer in downtown Lake Elsinore. Williamson was stunned because she clearly remembered seeing Mr Nazarowski in her past vision of Civil War-era Virginia!

A short while later, Williamson realized that the woman who was her editor at the newspaper, Barbara Roberts, was also a former Millboro past-life resident. In fact, she knew with certainty that her editor was her mother-in-law in her previous life.

This was getting just too strange!

Maureen Williamson thought she might be going over the edge somehow. On the other hand, she didn't feel unhinged. This all seemed like normal, matter-of-fact knowledge. She had clearly seen Nazarowski and Roberts in her past life regression images, of that she had no doubt. It came with the certainty of 'just knowing'.

There was one way however to find out if she wasn't just getting carried away. Williamson wondered if her fellow Lake Elsinore residents could also be regressed - without telling them the details of what she knew and experienced - to see if they also remembered lives in Millboro.

Maureen Williamson and Dr Marge Rieder asked Joe Nazarowski if he would agree to undergo hypnotic past-life regression. A straight-laced sceptic, Nazarowski couldn't imagine why he was being approached with such an offer. At first, he refused - he was a total non-believer. He was an atheist who didn't belief in an afterlife or even heaven or hell. He was of the opinion that reincarnation was impossible, and the complete and utter nonsense of gullible New Agers.

However, Nazarowski finally agree to be hypnotized - but only because he wanted a free session to help him quit smoking. Dr Rieder agreed to address his nicotine habit with hypnotism, and got his permission to suggest that he reach further back in time, just as an experiment, to see if he could recall a past life.

Under hypnosis, Joe Nazarowski easily slipped back through time and found himself in the body of a man whose name was Charles F. Patterson. He was a high-ranking military officer and graduate of West Point. He was a contemporary of General George Armstrong Custer, and knew the famous general well enough to have put molasses in his shoe as a prank. And yes, Nazarowski confirmed that Charles F. Patterson had been a resident of Millboro, Virginia.

Even after his regression, Nazarowski still considers himself a sceptic, although he says he simply cannot explain the certainty he felt about the many details he could remember of his life as Charles. F. Patterson. But what really floored Nazarowski was what came next.

Marge Rieder decided to do some research. She travelled to Salt Lake City, Utah, to search the massive collection of genealogical records stored at the Family History Center of the Church of Jesus Christ of Latter Day Saints. Reader, please remember that this was still the early 1990s before the Internet became what it is today. Searching genealogical records is easily done now with a few strokes of the keyboard, but before the Internet, the task was far more difficult. One of the best options for anyone living in any American state was a visit to Salt Lake City, where massive paperbound records of millions of family histories from all over the nation are stored. The Church of Latter Day Saints collects such data for religious reasons, although we won't go into such detail here.

Searching the massive Salt Lake City archives, Rieder was able to locate a man by the name of Charles Patterson, born and raised in Millboro, Virginia, and who fought in the American Civil War.

Upon learning of the reality of Charles Patterson, and comparing this with his vivid hypnotic recall of the man, Nazarowski reached an impasse with himself. Now he had to admit that the situation was, in his words:

"Not all nuts."

While he maintains a level of disbelief, he stated:

"The facts here are simply indisputable."

Williams recognized other Lake Elsinore residents as

past-life residents of Millsboro - including her own husband, Ralph Williamson. He was a man, one of several apparently, with whom she had an affair with as Rebecca Ashford.

Marge Rieder and Maureen Williamson were able to identify at least two dozen people in California who had past lives in Millboro. They in turn recognized even more. As more people were uncovered, further evidence to prove that this was a real case of reincarnation was made possible.

For example, one of the 'regressed' people recalled that although Millboro was a town in Confederate territory, and therefore pro-slavery, there was a hidden sanctuary within the village where runaway slaves could temporarily hide on their way to freedom in the North.

Again most people, including historians in Millboro, declared this to be certain nonsense. No such sanctuary for slaves was ever uncovered or documented in Millboro. After the Civil War ended with a Union victory, freeing the slaves, there was still no mention or revelations about a hidden safe house.

However, the person who recalled the secret sanctuary was able to provide exacting information about where it was, what it looked like, how big it was, and more. The secret hiding place for runaway slaves would be found underground near a small church. It would have green plaster walls and the dimensions of the room would be such and such. In fact, this person remembered that the underground room was part of a larger structure of several subterranean chambers originally constructed by Indians. There were a number of connecting rooms and tunnels.

Marge Rieder travelled to Millboro and obtained

permission to dig at the location where the underground slave sanctuary was said to be located by the reincarnational memory. Donning a pair of work gloves and boots and armed with only a spade, this elderly woman started hacking away at the rocky topsoil. Using what she learned from books about basic archaeological methods, she began excavating a narrow trench, hoping to run into a secret underground chamber beneath the well-trodden surface of the two century old community of Millboro.

She found what she was looking for - an underground room that had the exact odd kind of green coloured plaster just as described by her hypnosis subject.

Local historians were stunned. Absolutely no records in any archive, museum or historic study, or even archaeological study, knew of any underground chambers where escaping slaves were housed. Local experts agreed that digging for such a site was ludicrous - until it was found - and using only the past-life memories of people regressed by hypnotic therapy.

There are other interesting factors which make this case of group reincarnation even more tantalizing. For example, when Maureen Williamson first recalled the name of the Virginia town where she lived in a past life, she pronounced it Marlboro like the famous cigarette brand. Other people who were subsequently regressed also pronounced the name of their town Marlboro.

It was this pronunciation and the Marlboro spelling that Marge Rieder used when first searching for the town in Virginia - but found nothing in the location where it should have been. By chance she saw the name of a village called Millboro. Since that was the closest to the name her patients had been using, she flew to the east coast and visited Millboro and discovered that most people pronounce the name of their town as Marlboro using their unique southern drawl, or dialect.

To date, more than fifty people now living in Lake Elsinore believe they had previous lives in Millboro, Virginia.

Dr Marge Rieder once regressed a roomful of those with past-life memories from Millboro. She put them all under simultaneously, asked them to embody their past-life personality, and then speak to each other as the people they once were.

The results were fascinating - and partially so because these long dead people picked up on their lives where they left off. That is, they discussed both issues of importance of their day, but also engaged in petty arguments. They talked of major and minor issues pertinent to the life of 1860s Millboro. It was as if more than a century had never passed and they were given a chance to live again.

The case of the Lake Elsinore-Millboro case is perhaps the most thoroughly documented case of group reincarnation in history. The evidence that was uncovered, including dozens of verifiable details checked out by many visits to Millboro, makes this an almost airtight example for the reality of reincarnation.

It also implies something amazing: That literally an entire community of individual souls can somehow all agree to come back to earth after they have died - and all return to the same location. But why choose a small town in California for the next go around? How are these decisions made by the individual souls? One must assume that all of these people - their souls - met at some mutual location in the afterlife, and that they all sat down, perhaps for a conference, to plan their next life.

There are countless examples of other group reincarnation cases, but on a much smaller scale. For example, members of a family have discovered that they once knew each other in a previous life. In a family of five, for example, it is often discovered that all five of these people knew each other in previous lives - but that they all played different roles. The mother and father may have been the children in the previous life. The wife may now be the husband, or the daughter, or the son, and so on.

Again, the implications are enormous when considering the true nature of reality - the reality of who and what we are. According to the reincarnation scenario, all of us have lived both as men and women. All of us have embodied lives of different races, nationalities and sexual orientations. We seem to be experimenting with experiencing every kind of human incarnation we can to learn as much as we can.

Dr Marge Rieder went on to write three books about the Millboro case: Mission to Millboro and Mission to Millboro: A Study in Group Reincarnation and Millboro and More. Sceptics have struggled to explain away the virtual mountain of incontrovertible evidence that has resulted from Rieder's investigations.

About the best that most sceptics can come up with is that they all just made the thing up. Others accused Dr Rieder of orchestrating the whole story by 'leading the witness' so to speak. They said she consciously, or unconsciously, planted the Millboro suggestion into the minds of her subjects - causing them all to buy into and believe the same invented story.

But it seems that Marge Rieder did just the opposite. For

example, after the fame of the story grew, many other Lake Elsinore residents also came to believe they had lived past lives in Millboro. Through hypnosis, Rieder was able to help most of them conclude they were mistaken - often to their disappointment. So, if anything, Rieder disabused people from the notion of their own reincarnation more often than she uncovered an actual member of this strange, but select group.

What sceptics simply cannot explain is how a person in California, who has never been to Virginia, could know about a secret underground chamber with green plaster walls - something even the people of Millboro never knew about their own town - and many other verified details of historic fact.

The Millboro case remains a source of wonder. Now, a quarter of a century later, the case has never been debunked by even the hardest working sceptics. It seems it is a remarkable bona fide case of not just reincarnation - but group reincarnation.

The Druze

The members of one of the most mysterious and obscure religious groups in the world are native to the mid-east countries of Syria, Israel, Jordon and Lebanon, but they are not Jewish, Muslims or Christians - and yet, they are somewhat all of the above.

They are known to history as the Druze. This group incorporates elements of the three major religions, but is also heavily influenced by Gnosticism, Neoplatonism and Pythagoreanism. There is one aspect of their belief system that is especially important to them - reincarnation.

It is estimated that there are fewer than seven hundred thousand Druze worldwide, although their faith is ancient, dating back to at least the 7th Century. The term 'Druze' is derived from the name of a man, Ad-Darazi, who is believed to have founded the religion, although he was later banished from the movement he helped create. Essentially, he wound up on the wrong side of an internal political struggle within the group. Perhaps because history is written by the victors, Ad-Darazi is considered a heretic among the modern Druze. He was executed about one thousand years ago in Egypt in the year 1018.

Thus, although historians and scholars today call them the Druze (also Druse) the secretive members of this mysterious faith prefer to call themselves the Muwaḥḥidū, which translates roughly as 'monotheism'. The precept that there is only one true God is a critical element for the Druze. They say that the Adam of the Bible was not the first man, but rather the first man to accept the idea of monotheism.

The Druze consider the Koran a sacred text, but they think of it merely as an 'outer shell' of a greater truth. Many Druze live in Israel, and are fiercely loyal citizens and supporters of Israeli policy - making many to mistakenly believe that the Druze are a Jewish sect. Others live in Syria, however, where they are generally taken as an offshoot or sect of Islam, similar to the Sufi. For the Druze, loyalty to one's country is held in high regard, no matter what the prevailing religion of that country, although they hold to their own belief system.

The Druze are mysterious in many ways. They even have a strict level of secrecy within their own ranks. For example, only a select few are allowed to know the true 'inner precepts' of the religion, while the rank-and-file Druze are kept in the dark - which they accept. The Druze have a self-regulated internal hierarchy. Some are 'elite' and 'in the know' but most are not.

But all of the Druze maintain a central relationship with what they call 'the Notq'. This is basically their word for reincarnation, but they also call those people who seem born with natural and powerful past-life memories 'the Notq'. About a third of Druze are of the Notq.

Stories of reincarnation abound among the Druze, but one such case recently uncovered is so amazing it captured national media attention. The story was first documented by a German researcher and therapist by the name of Trutz Hardo. The story was picked up by the Epoch Times, an international news organization based in China. The Epoch Times is a respected multimedia platform, from print to broadcast and Internet, and has won many national awards for unbiased coverage and solid journalism around the world.

On 17 May 2014, the Epoch Times ran the story of a

three year old boy living in the Golan Heights, an area controlled by Israel, although claimed as legal territory by Syria. Israel took control of the Golan Heights after the 1967 war and has since refused to relinquish control of the land.

The Golan Heights boy was born with a long red birthmark across the top of his head. This was an immediate sign to his Druze family that their new son was of the Notq. Like many mainstream researchers believe today, birthmarks can be a strong indicator of a previous life - they usually indicate a site of severe trauma to the body of the previous-life individual, and this wound is what probably ended their life.

In fact, all Druze examine their newborns thoroughly for birthmarks.

The boy had already developed good language skills by three years of age. One of the first things he began to speak of was his belief that he had been murdered by an axe blow to the head. He also remembered the village where this event took place.

Because reincarnation is a central tenet of their religion, the Druze take all such reports as extremely important - in fact, they believe it is almost mandatory that they investigate such accounts. And so the parents decided to take their son to the village he remembered. As soon as they arrived, the location stimulated the boy's memory and he recalled his name in his previous life. It didn't take long before they found someone who knew the man in question - and said that the whereabouts of this person was a mystery - because he had gone missing four years ago.

The little boy said:

"He is not missing! He is dead! I was that man! I was

murdered with an axe!"

Incredibly, as more information was uncovered, the boy began to remember even more, including the name of the murderer. This accused killer was still a resident of the small community. Based on the boy's remarkable past-life memories, village elders agreed to confront the man in question.

When hearing the charges, local observers said that the man's eyes bulged and his face turned white - yet, he denied having anything to do with the brutal axe murder. However, new revelations from the small boy were beginning to spill forward at a rapid rate, further implicating the man. Still, it was all highly circumstantial.

But then the boy delivered the nail in the coffin. He said he could recall exactly where his body had been secretly buried. Authorities went to the location and after excavating a shallow grave, they found the skeleton of a man, and the skull had been bashed in with what was obviously a sharp-edged instrument of some kind. In case there was any doubt left, an axe was found buried near the body.

After all the evidence had come out, the man confessed to the murder.

All of these events - the boy's return to the village, his memories, the confrontation of the suspect, the exhumation of the body - were witnessed and documented by Dr Eli Lasch, a famous doctor of impeccable credentials. He is the man who developed the medical system for Gaza as part of a large-scale Israeli government improvement project. He died in 2009, among the most famous of all Israeli medical professionals.

Thus, it cannot be said that the amazing case of the Druze boy was a tale concocted by gullible people who belonged to an obscure cult-like religion, and who were all too willing to tailor facts to fit a preconceived belief system.

Furthermore, when the skull of the dead man was examined, the wound in the head almost exactly matched the birthmark of the boy who said he has was this man in a previous life. By all measures, the case of the reincarnated Druze boy is an iron-clad case for the reality of reincarnation.

The issue of birthmarks alone tends to be a major point of verification in reincarnation cases. Another example is the following account which was also originally uncovered by Trutz Hardo, and was investigated by one of the premier reincarnation investigators, Dr Ian Stevenson who worked at the School of Medicine at the University of Virginia.

The case has many striking similarities with that of the Druze boy of the Golan Heights.

In the small Turkish village of Hatun Köy, a boy named Semih Tutusmus told his parents that Semih was not his real name. He began insisting so as soon as he could speak well enough at about the age of four. He said his real name was Selim Fesli, and that he had been murdered by a neighbour of their village.

Semih has been born with a strangely shrunken and deformed ear. When he began to speak of his past life, he said that he was murdered by being shot with a rifle in the right ear. He soon remembered the name of the man he once was, and other details about his previous life. His former life was in the same village of Hatun Köy.

At four years of age, Semih took it upon himself to walk

to the home of the deceased Selim Fesli. He knocked on the door and announced to the widow of Selim:
"I am Selim, you are my wife Katibe."
Katibe was stunned, of course, but as she continued to speak with little Semih, it was clear that he knew an astonishing number of details about the life and family of the deceased Selim Fesli. Katibe also confirmed dozens of details that only she and her husband could have known.
It wasn't long before Semih recalled more details of the death of Selim. It seems that he was shot by a neighbour, a man by the name of Dirbekli. This man had claimed that the incident had been purely accidental. But Semih said it had been premeditated murder, precipitated by a dispute over grazing land for Selim's mule. Dirbekli continued to deny this version of events, however, and was never charged with a crime.
Due to the failure of authorities to accept that the death of his former self had been a murder, little Semih developed a grudge. The boy would sometimes throw rocks at Dirbekli when he encountered him in their small village, or shout curses at him. Although his parents and others could understand his motivation, a child treating an elder in this manner was considered scandalous. There was nothing else to do other than to try to convince the boy to cease this behaviour. A local village elder persuaded Semih that if he continued to persecute the man whom he believed killed him in a previous life, it would set up an endless cycle of conflict and revenge. He told Semih that when Dirbekli died, he might then reincarnate as well and visit persecution upon Semih in this life.
As Semih grew older, he accepted that his former life as Selim was gone. He came to understand that it was his

current life that was important, and that he must make the most of it. Living a good life was the only way that negative Karmic entanglements could be alleviated, no matter who was at fault.

The case of Semih Tutusmus is yet another example where a variety of evidential factors come together to make a powerful circumstantial case that the mechanics of reincarnation are at play. Some say the facts are more than circumstantial. They think that the deformed ear Semih Tutusmus was born with is an almost undeniable connection and direct evidence of the way Selim Desli was killed by Dirbekli. That, combined with the detailed knowledge of a four year old boy about the life of Selim, makes for an intriguing body of evidence supporting the reality of reincarnation.

The Evidence of the Druze
The rich tradition of reincarnation among the Druze is what originally attracted the attention of Dr Ian Stevenson of the University of Virginia, who searched the world for the most striking cases of reincarnation. As we said, Stevenson was a pioneer in this field and was perhaps the first qualified academic with a respected scientific background who dared to look further into what could be considered an 'occult' subject in modern western nations.

After Dr Stevenson learned of the Druze traditions, he travelled to Lebanon in the late 1970s. He walked unannounced into a Druze village and began asking local residents if they knew of any families where children spoke of past lives. Many immediately referred him to a boy by the name of Imad Elawar.

This boy began using complex language very early in his

life and could speak by the age of one. His very first words were two names: Jamileh and Mahmoud.

At the age of two, Imad broke away from his mother to run up to a man in the streets whom he said had once been his neighbour. Using this as a starting point, Dr Stevenson located an area on the other side of the village where the boy had claimed to live in his previous life and he planned to take the boy back to see what he could remember. But before the visit, Stevenson worked closely with Imad, asking him to recall as many specific details as possible about the neighbourhood in which he believed he once lived before.

Stevenson compiled a list of fifty-seven items of information which he determined would be verifiable, but also impossible for the boy to learn or fake in any way. A subsequent investigation enabled Stevenson to verify fifty-one of the fifty-seven items. These included:

*He discovered that the name 'Mahmoud', which was among the first words that Imad spoke, turned out to be the name of his uncle in his previous life.

*He also found that the name 'Jamileh' was the name of a woman whom he had fallen in love with in his previous life.

*Stevenson tracked down the secret location of a rifle that Imad had cleverly hidden in the home of the man of his previous life, and which no one else knew about.

*Imad correctly identified his former self in a photograph, and also correctly identified another photograph of a man who was his brother. He recalled his brother's name and that of other family members.

*In one amazing situation, Stevenson sat in on a conversion between the toddler Imad and an older man whom he said he had been in military service with during his previous life. The boy and the man recounted numerous experiences they had whilst in the army.

Dr Stevenson published his findings among the Druze in a 1978 academic paper which remains among the best pieces of scientific research validating the reality of reincarnation.

Today the Druze are a small population representing a unique culture which is experiencing perhaps the most dangerous era of its millennium long existence. Extremists in Syria are persecuting and murdering any group - including offshoots of Islam, such as the Sufi - who are considered heretical to Islam from their extremist viewpoint.

The Druze are a primary target for those who consider this rare culture to be heretical. Because of their small numbers, the Druze and their unique culture and special relationship with reincarnation are in danger of vanishing or, at the very least, having their numbers and culture scattered across the globe.

The Genius Connection

Many people believe the best explanation for childhood genius is reincarnation.

But the same explanation is sometimes invoked for people who achieve greatness later in life – and sometimes these giants of history are the ones to make the claim that they have been here before.

But first, let us look at a remarkable six year old boy who recently made news across Great Britain and was also featured in a 27 February 2013 front page story by the Jamaica Times.

The boy is Joshua Beckford, born of Jamaican parents but adopted at four years of age by Knox Daniel of South Tottenham, England. Mr Daniel began to suspect that his son was special when the boy started to speak in complete sentences before the age of one. It seems that he taught himself to read signs in the supermarket by the age of two. Knox Daniel was stunned when this two year old toddler began calling out the names of food products and advertisements while shopping.

By the age of six, Joshua was certified a genius, having scored off the charts on an IQ test.

He was accepted to study philosophy at Oxford in a special programme for children aged eight to thirteen. Although only six years old, an exception was made for Joshua and he finished the programme with distinction, easily staying with his 'much older' classmates.

By eight years of age, Joshua was already well on his way to mastering two foreign languages - Japanese and Mandarin Chinese. He now speaks both fluently. He also has a keen interest in human anatomy and has successfully performed simulated surgeries on the human brain. One of his goals is to become a neurosurgeon. He is also deeply interested in Egyptology and is nearing completion of his first children's book on the subject. He is a wizard at mathematics, and all other subjects of basic education.

Joshua is also convinced he is reincarnated, even though the man he was in his former life was more ordinary. Joshua says he has definite past-life memories of being a soldier who was killed on the battlefield. The memory of his death is so powerful that Joshua is determined to find a way to manipulate DNA in way that will 'switch off' the aging process, and possibly death itself.

Joshua has also been diagnosed with a form of autism, a trait often associated with genius abilities.

Some say the fact that Joshua remembers a previous life has little bearing on the genius he is today, especially since his past-life memories would seem to have few similarities to his current life. And yet, the suggestion of a connection is there.

There are many other cases, however, where a direct connection between a past life of great accomplishment and a present life of genius is undeniable. A superb illustration of this is the case of Dr Norm Shealy.

The Doctor Returns

Norm Shealy began telling everyone that he was going to be a doctor when he was four years old. Few doubted this because the child was a prodigy, or nearly so. He was brilliant across the educational board, excelling in maths, science, history and the study of languages.

He was allowed to enter college at the age of sixteen to study human biology as he was determined to become a neurosurgeon. He finished his undergraduate studies and was accepted into one of the best medical schools in the United States, Duke University, at the age of nineteen. He breezed through medical school and after being awarded his medical degree, the young Dr Shealy began on a remarkable career of groundbreaking discovery.

Dr Shealy specialized in the relief of pain. His first major invention was the TENS unit, a device which distributes electrical charges through the skin to block pain. He also invented the Dorsal Column Stimulator, a device that places electrodes near key points in the spinal cord that will block pain signals from getting to the brain. His next development was a surgical breakthrough, a procedure called Facet Rhizotomy, which is a safe way to cut highly sensitive nerve endings near the spine that transmit pain.

In 1972 Dr Shealy was attending a lecture at the Neuroelectric Society in Colorado when a speaker mentioned the name of an 18th Century British physician who was a pioneer in the use of hypnotism as a way to perform surgery on people without excessive pain. The British doctor's name was John Elliotson and as soon as Dr Shealy heard this name, his world changed.

Dr Shealy said he immediately felt as if someone had thrust an iceberg down his back. He said afterwards that at that point he had an immediate sense of knowing and as he walked out of the conference in a daze, a thought came into his head. He said to himself:

"Dr John Elliotson, my God, that's me!"

Before this unexpected encounter, Dr Shealy had never given reincarnation a single thought. He had been busy in the world of medicine, conducting pure science and research and treating patients on the operating table. But now something astounding seemed to have come crashing into his life - the certainty that he had lived before as another doctor in the previous century.

After the conference Dr Shealy attempted to find historical data on Dr John Elliotson, but there was very little information. He was determined to find out more, so he travelled to England where he hoped to track down the life of the man he now seemed to remember as being himself.

Once in London, Dr Shealy hailed a cab and asked to be driven to the Royal College of Surgeons, assuming Elliotson had been a surgeon, and thus records of his work and life should be found there. Driving through the busy streets of London, Shealy's driver happened to pass by the University College Hospital of London, and again he felt the 'iceberg on his back'. He turned around and looked at the venerable building and knew instantly that this was where Dr John Elliotson had kept his office in the 1800s. Dr Shealy told his driver to stop the car and as he got out and walked into the hospital, aspects of his life as John Elliotson immediately became known to him. He said it was as if he had returned to a familiar home.

A subsequent investigation into the life of Dr Elliotson uncovered an amazing number of similarities between the two men. Like Shealy, Dr Elliotson had been a pioneer in the treatment of pain. Elliotson was among the first to use narcotics to assist surgery, and also hypnotism to reduce or eliminate pain. Again, like Shealy, Elliotson was the first to adopt groundbreaking medical devices, including the use of the stethoscope.

Both men became disenchanted with much of what happens in mainstream medicine, and both wrote books decrying the 'hypocrisy of modern medicine'. In the days of Dr Elliotson, hypnotism (then called mesmerism) was considered to be fringe science and smacked of the occult. Even though Dr Elliotson found that it worked perfectly in hundreds of surgical procedures, Britain's medical community never accepted it.

Dr Shealy is also an advocate today of many natural healing techniques that are widely criticized and not accepted by mainstream science. He has developed a number of products, from aromatic oils and electronic treatments of 'power points' along the human body which he says can relieve pain and heal far more effectively than drugs or invasive surgical techniques.

There are other small points of confluence between the lives of the two doctors, separated by a century. For example, John Elliotson had black curly hair, and Norm Shealy had always felt that his own hair was somehow 'wrong'. In fact, just before leaving for his first day of medical school, he had dyed his hair black and had it curled - although later abandoned the practice because it was too time consuming.

Both men had a peculiar but powerful dislike of wearing knickers. It was common in the 18th Century for young men in England to wear knickers, and this was also the case in 1930s South Carolina where Shealy was born in 1932. Both young men adamantly objected to wearing knickers from an early age.

Both men walked with a limp. Dr Elliotson was afflicted with a congenital condition which produced a slight limp as he grew to adulthood. Norm Shealy fractured a tibia bone which became infected, resulting in a permanent limp throughout the rest of his life.

Finally, photographs of Dr John Elliotson compared side to side with Dr Norm Shealy show faces that are strikingly similar.

Once again, note that Norm Shealy is widely considered to have been a 'medical child prodigy'. Not only did he begin declaring his intention to be a doctor at four years old, but he could also read and write by that age, and was developing a deep understanding of the sciences, especially biology.

Today Dr Shealy himself has no doubt that reincarnation is a fact, and that he lived before as a maverick physician in London. He returned to practice again, determined to widen the art of healing beyond the 'materialism' of science, and by recognizing that all people are more than their physical bodies, meaning we can tap into nonphysical means to heal illnesses.

The Boy Surgeon
In the remote village of Himachal Pradesh in India, local residents have no doubt that Akrit Jaswal is the product of reincarnation. In the year 2000 he performed his first medical surgery at the age of seven on a girl who was one year older than he, being eight years old.

The story was covered in depth by journalist Cosmo Landesman of the British newspaper, The Sunday Times. Akrit was well prepared by the age of seven to perform surgery. That was because when he was four years old he had already finished reading Grey's Anatomy, absorbing a thorough knowledge of the human body. He was also allowed to observe surgical techniques by doctors at a local hospital.

A little girl from his village suffered a severe burn on her hand which left her with a cramped, closed fist and fingers jammed tightly together. She was in constant pain and her family was too poor to afford medical treatment. Akrit offered to perform surgery that would release her muscles, free her fingers and cure her pain - the operation was a complete success.

When asked if he was nervous during the operation, Akrit said:

"No, I wasn't. I have read many medical books and attended many operations. I think I did a better job than most surgeons. They would have opted for plastic surgery, but I didn't need to."

Like many child prodigies, Akrit began speaking by the age of one and reading by the age of two. By the time he was three years old he was tackling Shakespeare, but then soon discovered human anatomy, and became almost unusually absorbed with learning how the human body works. He was also interested in other aspects of human biochemistry. A short while after achieving fame for his successful surgery, Akrit announced that his mission in life would be to find a cure for cancer.

Akrit began attending Punjab University when he was eleven years old, and was also invited to London to meet with researchers at Imperial College. Medical researchers were eager to get his innovative perspective on oral gene therapy, which is an area of particular interest to him.

Akrit's genius has unfortunately lead to difficulties in his life. His highly public declaration that he would 'cure cancer' invited both unrealistic expectation and derision from some. His parents eventually divorced and his father was accused of milking his brilliant son's fame for money and publicity, robbing Akrit of a normal childhood.

Akrit denies this, and even calls it ridiculous. He said he has enjoyed all the normal experiences of childhood.

Some experts have also noted that although Akrit's IQ is in the genius range, he is normal or below normal in certain areas of learning.

Today Akrit is a student of biology, zoology and chemistry and plans to attend Harvard.

Of course, the local Hindi culture that Akrit Jaswal was born into is steeped in the concept of reincarnation and so ironically this aspect of his amazing abilities has been understated. In other words, when a child such as Akrit emerges seemingly from the womb with advanced abilities, it is just naturally assumed that reincarnation is at play.

When the same phenomenon occurs in other cultures however, such as in the case of American Dr Norm Shealy, the reincarnational connection uncovered by Dr Shealy takes on a vivid contrast with society norms.

Is it Proof of Reincarnation?

Of course, there are many cases of childhood genius wherein the gifted youngster has no past-life memories, or at least the gifted person never makes mention of such. But many argue that there simply is no better explanation for a child born with advanced talents.

One of the most commonly cited examples from history is the case of Mozart who composed his first sonata by the age of four and wrote a complete opera by the age of eight. These were not works of mere childlike quality, but had all the flavour of works produced by a mature composer.

Mainstream sceptics would say that some children are just born with brains that work remarkably fast, and are somehow genetically superior to the majority of the population. But as to the 'how' of why a brain works at a superior rate - well, there simply is no explanation for that. To say that genius children are simply born with 'superior brain power' is not a sufficient explanation. It is a theory with no mechanical details, yet sceptics grasp at it eagerly because anything is better for them than acknowledging the perfectly good explanation of reincarnation.

Additionally, even a superior brain would not explain how some children have skills and abilities that their supposed 'super brains' had no time to learn. In other words, they possess skills they were never exposed to. So it would make no difference if their brains are superior or not - the abilities they have seem to have been 'front end loaded' upon birth - and the source of that loading can be logically explained by memories obtained from a previous life. This is more than a theory because as we have seen in the case of Dr Norm Shealy and many others, they have direct experience of exactly that. Not only do they remember previous lives, but they have gone further to find direct evidence that they share many of the same traits, skills, talents and interests as the previous life they remember.

Sceptics, of course, will never buy the argument, but that won't stop genius children from being born and coming into the world with advanced talents they had little or no time and opportunity to learn the old fashioned way. Furthermore, the case for a reincarnation connection is bolstered when the child has definite past-life memories. In the latter case, it seems there is only one logical and reasonable conclusion - that skills learned in a past life can survive death and reappear in the life of a new person.

The Science of Reincarnation

The New York Times called him 'one of today's three most important living scientists'.
And if you ask this brilliant man about reincarnation, he says that it is not only a possibility, but almost certainly a reality.
His name is Dr Robert Lanza, and he is among a growing list of the world's most advanced thinkers who now say that reincarnation not only makes sense scientifically, but it would be surprising if life did not go on after we die. More and more mainstream science is coming to the conclusion: We never die. When we leave this body, we will live again.
Lanza is among a cadre of cutting edge scientific innovators who say it's time to stop thinking of the biological human brain as the source of consciousness. Rather, Lanza says that consciousness is sourced from outside the human brain. The brain is perhaps closer to a 'receiver' and 'tuning' device that is immersed in a universal field of consciousness. Consciousness is encoded data existing as electromagnetic energy that can never be degraded or destroyed. It's out there - it's all around us. We're swimming in it.
Lanza says that consciousness is the primal base that makes up the universe.
Born in Boston in 1956, Lanza can be said to have been a child prodigy. As a boy he conducted experiments in his basement involving the biology of chickens. He found a way to alter the genetic structure of chicken cells. The results of these experiments were brought to the attention of scientists at Harvard Medical School. Lanza was

invited to consult with such giants of medical research as Dr Jonas Salk, the man who cured polio, and Christian Bernard, the man who performed the first heart transplant. Both men mentored Lanza as he proceeded to earn a medical degree.

The list of accomplishments acquired by Dr Lanza are almost too numerous to mention here, but they include being involved in the development of the first cloned human embryos. He was among the first to generate stem cells from adults using something called somatic-cell nuclear transfer. Lanza was the first man to clone an endangered species, a type of bull known as a gaur.

Today Dr Lanza is Chief Science Officer to Ocata Therapeutics, a cell technology company. He is also Professor of Regenerative Medicine at Wake Forest University School of Medicine.

In 2007 Dr Lanza released a paper which outlined what he calls his theory of 'Biocentrism' and expanded on the concept in his 2009 book, Biocentrism: How Life and Consciousness are the Keys to Understanding the Universe.

In this book Dr Lanza makes a case that the very structure of the universe is made up of laws, forces, energies and constants that clearly show how intelligence, or the mind, exists before matter. That is, the brain does not generate consciousness. It is the other way round. Our 'minds' and 'personalities' are not trapped inside the 'meat' of our brains, and consciousness is flowing into the brain and through it.

Lanza calls space and time 'tools of our animal understanding'. We carry space and time around with us 'like turtles with shells' - meaning that when our shell wears out and we cast it off, we're ready to don a new shell to have another go at physical-biological life.

Dr Lanza says that human beings as a species have developed the wrong idea about what death is because we have become confused about the nature of biological reality. He says we are too 'biocentric' thinking biology and physical matter are everything. We have come to identify solely with our physical bodies based on that which we see in the mirror every day, what we feel (be it pain or pleasure) and so on. But all of these sensations are not 'coming from within' but are being transmitted 'from without'.

Dr Lanza is boldly acknowledging what the vast majority of today's material scientists have long refused to do - that one must take into account the quantum nature of physical reality when considering the human body's place in the universe. He is attempting to show how the physical body interlaces with all of the non-physical energies that are swirling all around us at every moment.

Support from a Physicist

NASA physicist Tom Campbell is onboard with the idea that reincarnation is not only possible, but a certainty.

Campbell has enjoyed a long career working at the very top of his field as a physicist and computer expert for the highest-tier clients - including U.S. Missile Defense firms and NASA. In fact, it was Campbell's work that helped the American fleet of space shuttles get back into orbit after two catastrophic explosions which had killed all on board. Campbell's work on statistical risk analysis gave NASA engineers the information they needed to bring back a level of flight safety that would enable the U.S. to return to space.

When Campbell was not working twelve hour days in the

aerospace industry, he was leading a kind of second life, exploring the more esoteric world of subjects that are taboo to mainstream science. This included such phenomenon as out-of-body travel, remote viewing and the non-local nature of consciousness. Campbell was instrumental in the early development of the Monroe Institute, which is among the leading consciousness exploration organizations in the world today.

Along with an electrical engineer in a crude laboratory set up in an old mobile home, Campbell conducted experiments for Monroe using specific sound frequencies which, when fed to the human brain, could be shown to produce transcendent states of mind, such as out-of-body experiences or deep states of meditation that might otherwise take Zen monks decades to achieve.

Over some thirty years of research, Campbell eventually produced a massive three volume series of books called My Big TOE with 'TOE' standing for 'Theory of Everything'.

In short, Campbell makes an extremely detailed scientific argument that consciousness is not generated by the brain - just the opposite - that consciousness comes first, and enters the brain only after a person is born and develops a biological body. The 'mind' of that person already exists, and could easily have inhabited another body in another time period.

Campbell presents a complex cosmology which describes our reality as a virtual reality. Life, Campbell says, is more like a gigantic computer. Our bodies are akin to avatars in a video game. Our true self - our consciousness - is no more 'inside' our physical bodies than the player of a computer game is inside the character in the game he or she is playing.

"What happens when your character in a video game gets killed by a dragon or a troll?" Campbell asks before answering:

"It just gets up again as soon as the player restarts the game. The avatar is not dead - its information is stored in the hard drive of the computer. It can be brought back to fight again another day."

One of Campbell's favourite phrases is:

It's all just data.

What he means is that everything we do, feel, see, taste and smell in our lives is essentially raw data that our biological brains are capturing from a kind of overarching 'supercomputer' that is generating a virtual reality scenario we find ourselves living within.

One of the questions many sceptics ask about the reincarnation scenario is this:

If people truly have immortal souls that never die, why do they have to enter physical bodies that live only for a few decades - usually less than a century - only to start all over again? Why can't this soul live five years, or a thousand years, rather than having to die every seventy-five to eighty-five years, or so?

Campbell says that lives partitioned into shorter spans make it easy for the soul to concentrate on learning specific lessons about life. The tendency is for most individuals to 'paint themselves into a corner' after a life of perhaps eight or nine decades. It's akin to a 'fruit that has ripened and now is ready to pick'. It's easiest to cash in all of the data collected in that lifespan, and then take a rest to evaluate everything that was learned. Once all the data is tabulated and sorted and meanings interpreted and understood, the soul can then rest before choosing its next go-around.

The Anesthesiologist

Another leading doctor who comes at this from yet another angle is Dr Stuart Hameroff who undertook his medical training at the Drexel University College of Medicine. His career in medical research was with the University of Arizona where he was a Professor in the Department of Anesthesiology and Psychology and Associate Director for the Center for Consciousness Studies.

Dr Hameroff's research led him to the study of microscopic cell structures called microtubules, which are components of the cytoskeleton which makes up cellular cytoplasm. This is the very basic structure of what human cells are made from at the most fundamental level.

Neurons or brain cells also have microtubule structures. They are so complex that Dr Hameroff realized that it was in these microscopic structures that the actual computation needed to produce conscious awareness takes place. Information is processed far below the atom or even subatomic level - and on the quantum level. Dr Hameroff says that the information being processed in the microtubules of the brain can leak out and connect directly to the surrounding universal field of consciousness. He argues that our experience of consciousness is the result of quantum gravity effects in these microtubules, a theory which he dubbed 'orchestrated objective reduction'.

Interestingly, another world-famous scientist came to precisely the same conclusion about microtubules working wholly independently of Dr Hameroff - it was Sir Roger Penrose, a British mathematical physicist, who is most famous for making major contributions to relativity theory and cosmology.

Penrose says that consciousness, or at least proto-consciousness, is a fundamental property of the universe, and it was present even at the first moment of the universe during the Big Bang.

"In one such scheme proto-conscious experience is a basic property of physical reality accessible to a quantum process associated with brain activity," Penrose said.

According to Penrose, our souls are constructed from the very fabric of the universe and may have existed since the beginning of time. Like Dr Lanza, Penrose says that our brains are just receivers and amplifiers for the proto-consciousness that is intrinsic to the fabric of space-time.

Dr Hameroff said in a recent TV documentary on the Science Channel:

"Let's say the heart stops beating, the blood stops flowing, the microtubules lose their quantum state. The quantum information within the microtubules is not destroyed, it can't be destroyed, and it just distributes and dissipates to the universe at large."

Hameroff said if the patient is revived, he or she may have a near-death experience. The person's 'quantum information' (or soul) would temporarily disassociate from the body and return when all systems return to normal. If the body dies, the quantum information is still viable and can be born, as in reincarnation, into a new life in a new time.

Full Circle

You might say we are living in the most amazing time in history. For centuries, science and mysticism have been at odds with each other on the most fundamental questions: What is life? What is consciousness?

About three hundred years ago, the total dominance of the materialist world view began with Isaac Newton who crystalized the idea of a 'billiard ball universe'. In Newton's view, all reality was made up of physical matter. His 'billiard balls' are what we came to call 'atoms' and these were seen as the most fundamental units of reality. No matter how 'alive' something seemed, the materialist point of view said there was no escaping the fundamental fact that everything is made up of basic building blocks of matter. That meant that what we experience as 'mind' or 'emotions' were basically illusions created by the interaction of 'dead stuff' which is temporarily put into motion by some form of energy. But when that energy is removed from the system, it falls apart and ceases to exist.

But just a little more than one hundred years ago quantum theory emerged. Furthermore, the atom proved not to be so solid and 'fundamental' after all. Break down an atom and you get electrons, neutrons and protons. These in turn can be broken down further into even more exotic particles, such as quarks, muons, bosons, neutrinos and more. It seems that no matter how far scientists attempted to break things down, there was always a deeper level.

We now recognize that an atom is 99.999999% empty space! All physical matter is basically an illusion created by the interaction of matter with energy. And as Einstein demonstrated, energy can never be destroyed. Energy can only be transformed to a new state. It can act as solid matter for a time, but then 'go back' or 'go on' to take on a purely flowing wavelike form of organized … something.

It was only a matter of time before biologists began to

consider the fact that the human body is made up of atoms, which in turn are made up of smaller and smaller particles, to the point that no physical matter reality can be found at all. Only energy is constant. That means that our human bodies are a form of pure energy as well ... and immortal.

Mystical and religious tradition had been holding this as fact all along, but because these forces had no way to prove what they were saying was true, it was relegated to the margins of society. Now, thanks to its former antagonist - science - mysticism has new ground upon which to stand.

Included in all of this is the concept of reincarnation.

Finally, what tens of thousands of people have been reporting based on their own direct experience or information accessed via hypnosis, can be validated as true.

Future-Life Reincarnation

The vast majority of the discussion about reincarnation centers on past lives.

People are curious to know: Did I live a century ago, five hundred years ago, or perhaps thousands of years ago in ancient times?

Do people who lived in previous centuries come back to walk among us today with new lives, new bodies, new personalities?

When people seek hypnotic regression, the therapist naturally guides people to 'go back in time' - in most instances they instruct the person to first go to their earliest memory of childhood, and then go even further – into the past.

But perhaps it was only a matter of time before some people began to think of the opposite. That is, instead of sending someone into the past, why not try to send them into the future?

Why not, indeed.

What has been emerging more recently in the reincarnation field is something called not 'REGRESSION therapy' but 'PROGRESSION therapy'. Instead of 'Regressing' a person into the past they seek to 'Progress' them into the future.

Just a few decades ago such a concept would have been much more difficult to grasp. That is because the majority of the population was working with a concept of time that was linear:

We are here in the present, everything behind us is in the past, and the future is yet to exist.

But enter quantum mechanics. Albert Einstein struck a

mighty blow against our old concept of time by proving scientifically that so much of what we observe about our universe is relative – including time. It seems time is not so immutable after all.

'Time,' Einstein said, 'is a kind of illusion.'

Einstein observed that time can speed up, or slow down, depending on your own speed and position. For example, people travelling in a spaceship going tens of thousands of miles per hour will experience a time slow down – although they won't observe it themselves.

But quantum theory was not finished restructuring the concept of time. Scientists began to model time as something that exists all at once. In effect, time is enfolded into a kind of singularity – into an ever present moment – the NOW. From the standpoint of the present, we can just as easily look to the past as we can the future.

Of course, this is what a number of ancient traditions have been saying for centuries, especially the various Buddhist philosophies which speak of the eternal present moment.

In recent decades, these concepts have filtered through to a larger part of society, thanks in part to the New Age movement which tends to take information from a variety of resources, be it from science or from religion, spirituality or … whatever.

So perhaps it was only a matter of time (no pun intended) that some experienced past-life regression therapists began guiding their subjects into the future.

One of the first major clues that people could go both backwards and forwards in time came out of near-death experience reports. Read how one of the most prominent and respected heart surgeons in the world, Dr Pim van Lommel of The Netherlands, described the general NDE experience:

'… people have the perception of being out-of-body and seeing their own body down there on the operating table, and they no longer have a connection with it, like they have taken off an old coat … then they see a light they are attracted to and they sometimes describe it as a tunnel … and then they can come into an other-worldly dimension with beautiful lights and beautiful landscapes and meeting a being of light and feeling incredible love, unconditional love, and all wisdom is there … and sometimes they can have a life review and they relive their whole life from early childhood … all of your memories are still there … and you are connected … you feel the emotions of other people in the past as well … and sometimes people can perceive future events as well, so they are in a dimension without time and without space, they are somewhere … in an ever-present moment … they also feel the emotions of others, they feel what will happen and they feel future events, which can be very disturbing because their present actions have future consequences …'

Lo and behold, near-death experiences not only seem to be legitimate, but also consistent with the latest models of quantum mechanics. The question is - is the ancient belief and direct experience with reincarnation consistent with the updated model of time, as well?

Near-Future Progression

Interestingly, therapists have already been using near-future progression for some time to help patients model their behaviors' and get an idea about what the future can be like so that they are able to make better decisions for their futures. This is usually a simple process of encouraging the patient to visualize what the next six months will be like, the next year, or perhaps the next five years. It is just the basic and familiar idea of planning and goal setting.

When performing this exercise while using a hypnotic technique, many people can not only very vividly visualize future events, but these events often take on a life of their own, so to speak. That is, the person is not simply inventing or creating a model of where they might be in six months, but a kind of spontaneous movie begins playing in their minds, as if they are witnessing actual future events.

A classic example comes by way of French therapist Dr Jamie Parque who used future progression hypnotism to help a woman he was treating to make a tough decision. The woman was married and had a small child, but her eight year marriage to her husband had long since grown cold. They had become distant from each other, their sexual attraction has long since waned and their daily basic interactions were strained.

The woman had recently met another man and was having an affair with him. She was now considering leaving her husband to take up a life with her new lover. She was worried about the effect on her child, however, and she was still uncertain about how well things would go with her new romantic interest.

Dr Parque progressed the woman to a point in time two years hence, and she found herself experiencing a highly realistic vision of being divorced and living with the new man in her life. The court had worked out joint custody for the child with her husband. She could vividly see herself living in an attractive apartment in a nearby city, and things seemed to be going generally well.

Her therapist then progressed her five years into the future, where the woman now found herself in an unhappy state. Her relationship with her former lover was over. He had left her for another woman. Her husband had also moved further away – to another country, in fact. This meant she was separated from her child for months at a time, and by a great distance. The result was a strained relationship with her only daughter. Taking a good look around in her five year future, she found herself in a deeply unhappy state.

Based on this experience, the woman decided to end the relationship with her lover and worked on repairing her existing marriage.

Far Future Progression

While sessions like the one described above are interesting enough and of genuine practical value, it wasn't long before more dramatic kinds of future progressions began to appear among the thousands of transcripts recorded by patients undergoing hypnotic therapy.

Just as many past-life regressions happened 'by accident' at first, future-life progressions also began to crop up spontaneously on the therapy couch.

One dramatic case is documented by writer Joseph Robert Cowles in his rather obscure book, Third Witness. In his book, Cowles produces the transcripts of a session that was intended to be a hypnotic regression into a past life, but spontaneously moved into a future life scenario. Cowles identifies the therapist as Alan Arthur Winston and the patient as Edward Peterson.

During the session Peterson, deep in trance, identified himself as a man named Albert who said he was born in a place called L5. When asked what or where L5 was,

Peterson said L5 was a space station orbiting the earth. He said that this space platform was positioned in a unique orbit – at that point in space where the gravity of the earth and the gravity of the moon basically reach an equilibrium. In this specific location in space, Albert (who liked to be called Al) said space objects could be maintained in a 'free ride' zone because the orbit of any object placed there would not decay and cause it to fall back to earth, or the moon.

As it happens, the concept of L5 has long been known by space scientists. The 'L' in L5 stands for Lagrange, the surname of 18th Century Italian astronomer Joseph-Louis Lagrange. He was the first to work out the mathematics describing the celestial mechanics influencing the interaction between three orbiting bodies. Lagrange established that there would be five Lagrange orbits between the earth, moon and the sun - L1, L2, L3, L4 and L5. Today there are a variety of artificial satellites installed at the various Lagrange points.

Winston claimed that his client knew nothing of astronomy and orbital mechanics going into the session, yet he was able to provide textbook descriptions of Lagrange points and how they worked.

But that was only the beginning.

Amazing Story

Peterson's future self began to weave a complex story of what life was like in his world, which was from one hundred and fifty years to two hundred years in the future. Peterson (as Al) said that he had been born on the L5 space station, and that he was the third generation. He had never been to earth, and neither had his parents or grandparents because the surface of the earth had been devastated by a nuclear war.

Al said that the bulk of humanity was now living in a series of space stations parked in Lagrange orbits. Each space station carried between ten thousand and thirty thousand people. Another surviving cadre of humanity was eking out a new existence on the moon and a smaller colony had been established on Mars, where some five hundred people were struggling to establish a foothold.

Al's story was rich in detail, and also peppered with highly technical data. His job was that of a miner working on the surface of the moon. His shift rotation was three weeks of digging rocks and minerals on the lunar surface, with one week of free time. He spent his off-week on the L5 station, which was his home.

Al said that the rocks he mined were processed for essential metals and minerals, and that oxygen was chemically extracted from the moon's regolith. There was also abundant water on the moon frozen in the form of the hydrogen isotope, H3. The metals and other precious elements were used for construction of underground tunnels on the moon, and to enhance and expand the space stations in the Lagrange orbits.

As for Mars, Al said that ancient pyramids and temple like structures from a long dead civilization had been discovered. Also, rare artefacts were sometimes found, including bracelets and necklaces that were extremely popular items among earth people. He called these 'do-dads'. Possession of a do-dad was much in demand.

Overall, however, society had been radically altered by the necessities of living on space stations and small planetary colonies. For example, there was no longer a monetary system and almost no one had (or really wanted) personal possessions, other than utilitarian basics such as clothing and the ordinary items that are a part of daily life. Al said:

'Why would anyone want money? What would you do with it? And what kind of things would you own? Where would you put them?'

Even so, Al said he did own one special possession – a collection of old books he had inherited from his grandfather. Paper and ink books were now relics of the past, of objects of curiosity at best. He considered these his most important belongings because of their personal meaning, and the only kind of thing that he might classify as a personal possession.

The earth was no longer called 'Earth' among the surviving remnants of space-bound humanity. They just called it 'the world'. Few held a desire to go there – in fact most people had never been on the surface of mankind's home world. A few stragglers actually still lived on earth, Al has explained, and they would occasionally visit the space stations or moon colony, but only under extremely tightly controlled conditions. This was because earth people might carry diseases, or they might be trouble makers, even terrorists.

Much of the surface of the earth had been rendered uninhabitable by nuclear war, but climate change had also devastated all of the cities located in coastal regions. A heated up planet had caused sea levels to rise, inundating cities like New York and Los Angeles, Sydney and Singapore – any world city in proximity of an ocean front.

Food on the moon and on L5 was grown in labs using soil mined from the moon reconditioned to support the growth of plants. Grow lights running on solar energy were a substitute for sunlight. There were even a few species of farm animals kept in space, although they were mostly chickens because they were small and reproduced rapidly, not to mention because they yielded a much needed source of protein-rich eggs.

What is truly convincing about Edward Peterson's account of his future life is the great technical detail he supplied - including the kind of things he could not have known about because he had no professional background in science or engineering.

The Future is Bright
Edward Peterson's future-life progression paints a rather dismal picture for the future of mankind, although the human race has clearly survived and is finding a way to start life anew. Some might find this a romantic or even an exciting adventure in a science fiction kind of way. Still, an earth devastated by war is not what most of us would hope for in the next century or two.

But can we conclude by the testimonial of one that his vision is the correct one? Not necessarily. That's because quantum scientists, new agers, mystics and psychics alike all agree that the future is not a single timeline as the past seems to be, but a multiple timeline or, more accurately, a field of probability futures. Before we discuss this important point further, let us look at what other future-life progression experiences report.

The Dystopian vision of Edward Peterson of life on a cramped space station seems to be the exception, by far. It is safe to say that there are now tens of thousands of future-life progressions on record, conducted by some of the most respected doctors, psychologists and therapists. The overwhelming majority of these describe future worlds that are positive, attractive, bright and sometimes even downright Utopian (albeit often after a century or two of strife).

The consensus seems to be this: The human race is heading towards a crisis phase that will play out over the next one or two centuries. The situation for the human race is going to get very difficult in coming decades due to overpopulation, environmental degradation and war. It seems that the collective nations of the earth are about to learn some extremely difficult lessons - but humanity will eventually emerge from this miserable experience thoroughly chastened, determined to turn away from its destructive ways, and ready to build a better world.

A tantalizing clue for this scenario comes from one of the most respected past-life regression experts, Dr Michael Newton. He has performed thousands of past-life regressions, many of which spontaneously move into future-life progressions. He had this to say with regards to future-life progression in a documentary film interview:

'I have had people who have been on starships because they are seeing into the future … a lot of times, though, I don't like working in the future when a client is able to talk to me about it because of the fact that I think from a karmic lesson's standpoint it's better that they do not know what's coming up … but I've had many clients talk to me about the 21st, 22nd Century, how overcrowded the next century is going to be on earth and how there is going to be a lot of air pollution and it's not going to be real easy living around here … in fact it's made my wife and I come to the conclusion that I think we'll wait a century before we reincarnate together again …'

More clues come from one of the most prominent practitioners of future-life progression, a dentist turned therapist and counsellor, Dr Bruce Goldberg. He is among the earliest to embrace the future-progression form of hypnotherapy. Dr Goldberg began progressing clients in 1977 and has worked with more than fourteen thousand individual clients over nearly four decades. In a recent television interview, Dr Goldberg said:

'I can tell you that the future is bright. Just about everyone who is able to retrieve memories of a future life reports beautiful worlds with marvellous societies based on peace and love and where everything anyone needs is provided for, almost automatically.'

Another example of this comes by way of a British hypnotherapist, Gordon Smith-Duran, who has a hypnotherapy practice in Darlington, a city in northeast England. In a remarkable YouTube video, Smith-Duran presents a regression-progression session with his teenage daughter, Jody. Smith-Duran first takes his daughter through a series of past lives, and then asks her to progress into the future to see if she can perceive a life yet to come.

Jody at first sees herself in an open field in a rural setting. She is a young woman wearing a skirt, a tunic and red shoes. The only structures she sees in her surroundings is a small farm house which belongs to her eighty year old grandmother. It is her impression that she is staying with her grandmother so that she can take care of her. Jody perceives that her name in this future life is Rebecca, and the year is 3020 - about one thousand years into the future.

Deep in hypnotic trance, Jody says she is simply running across the field but only because she is just so happy.

Her father extracts more information:

Jody, as Rebecca, says she is a student studying law at a

university which she describes as elaborately constructed of something like plastic and lots of windows. It's a beautiful structure, but so strange in appearance that proper words of description fail her. Her father then asks her to move to the point where she is about to die and leave this future-life incarnation. She sees herself as an elderly woman dying peacefully in bed after a long, serene life.

She then moves beyond her physical body into the spiritual realm. Her father asks her to sum up what that particular life was all about, and what she was to learn from it. Rebecca said:

'That not everything is bad; that you can live a happy life.'

This case is highly representative of thousands of other future-life progressions documented by such practitioners as Dr Bruce Goldberg and Dr Michael Newton, together with others working in the hypnotherapy field, such as prolific author Dolores Cannon, and many more.

All seem to find – in general – that future earth scenarios are of a planet at peace and developing in a more natural way. It's a serene world of mostly rural, bucolic and idyllic settings. But again, time and again, these more hopeful scenarios come only after a century or more of terrible strife precipitated by the path we are on today.

That path is a technology dominated society driven by dirty fossil and nuclear fuels, overconsumption, overpopulation, petro-chemical agriculture and governmental power structures that are becoming ever more controlling, oppressive and warlike. It's a vicious circle precipitated by a human species that feels the growing pressure of competition over dwindling resources and environmentally clean places to live, not to mention locations where tribal warfare and localized military strife and violent acts of terrorism are rampant.

Multiple Timelines

So now, let us return to that feature of future-life progression that distinguishes it sharply from past-life regression. Again, the past we remember and the past where our former lives played out, seems singular or monolithic – to put it simply, a one-way street. We all recognize the world we have come from, and that world is generally historically consistent.

But the future is quite different. All the scientific evidence points to a future that is not a single path forward, but a selection of infinite probabilities. No individual future timeline is set in stone. There are many. Not only are there many future timelines, but all of them may come into existence, and each will remain a solid reality existing side-by-side with an infinity of others.

That's why even the best psychics never make predictions about the future with one hundred percent accuracy. The problem is, we can never be certain which future is being looked at when probed with psychic abilities, scientific remote viewing, or future-life hypnotic progression.

The question for each of us is this: Which path do we want to go down? We have a choice based on the actions we select today shaped by the belief systems and values we adopt.

The good news seems to be that the future is not set in stone, no matter how bad things look today. We choose which path we are going to go down every time we take action and make a decision, both as individuals and collectively as a species. It seems that the kind of future we create is up to us. We can choose a future timeline that is bright, peaceful, loving and harmonious, or we can continue to go down a destructive path of materialism, abuse of nature, degradation of the oceans, rampant consumerism, waste, war, overpopulation, and more.

It is encouraging that the majority of future-life progression cases point to a bright future. Yes, there are the occasional examples – as we saw with the case of Ed Peterson and his bleak space station scenario – where the outlook is not so attractive at all. But if we are to believe the vast bulk of future-life progression data collected to date, the human race is not only destined to survive, but we may even create that idyllic Utopian scenario that so many still believe is possible – if only humanity will wake up, modify its behaviour and actively strive to create the kind of future world we so very much want for our children.

Book Two

12 Real Life Reincarnation Stories In The News

Contents

Book One iii

Introduction 7

Bentreshyt – A Priestess of Isis 11

The Reawakening of Marty Martin 21

Past Lives on Other Planets...31

The Interesting Case of Sherrie Lea Laird and Marilyn.................39

Life on Mars 49

Group Reincarnation 61

The Druze 71

The Genius Connection...81

The Science of Reincarnation 91

Future-Life Reincarnation...101

Book Two 115

Introduction 119

Dr Paul DeBell – Past Life Regression Therapy 123

Jeffrey Keene & The Civil War General 129

Samuel Helander & His Uncle Pertti 135

The Amazing Case of Uttara Huddar & Xenoglossy......141

Life Between Life 155

Split Reincarnation – One Soul, Many Lives 161

The British Carl Edon & The German Heinrich Richter 167

Suicide and Reincarnation 171

Maroczy (Deceased) v Korchnoi (Living) Chess Match 1985 177

Dolores Jay – Suggested Reincarnation? 185

The Spirit Guides 191

Conclusion 197

Introduction

Reincarnation is Among Our Most Ancient Beliefs, and Is Resurging in Modern Times

The people with the longest oral histories extending back into the mists of time are the Aboriginal tribes of Australia. Their myths and legends date back at least sixty thousand years. In these earliest of man's recorded history, we find a belief in reincarnation.

Harvard-educated cosmologist Paul Von Ward conducted extensive research of ancient cultures all over the world and reports that the idea of reincarnation is present in all of them - and from the very earliest records which date back tens of thousands of years.

It is interesting to note that reincarnation beliefs are found in all cultures on all continents, even among cultures that have never had contact with each other. Whether it be Native Americans in the West, or societies of the ancient Orient, the idea that the soul leaves the physical body, only to live again on this earth, is a universally present idea.

Most people know that the Hindu and Buddhist traditions consider reincarnation a major part of their religious structures – but did you know that this is also the case with the Inuit Indians of North America, that the Jewish faith accommodates reincarnation (in Hebrew: the gilgul ha'ne'shamot) and that even the Christian faith accepted reincarnation as dogma up until about fifteen hundred years ago? According to one survey, 24% of modern Christians accept reincarnation as either possible or fact. Reincarnation is found in hundreds of other religious belief systems as well.

What's interesting is that reincarnation is not one of those ancient ideas that has lost its cache of credibility as the world progressed into the modern age. Dozens of old superstitions have been dropped along the way, but not reincarnation. If anything, the belief in reincarnation has gained strength as science has advanced. That's because the scientific method can be applied to the study of actual cases of reincarnation, and the results are often tantalizing and, more often than not, support the reality of reincarnation.

The ways in which science and modern technology have added credibility to reincarnation are almost too numerous to mention, but just consider the invention of photography some one hundred and fifty years ago. For the first time, we have been able to compare pictures of the deceased to the reincarnated living - with results that are often stunning. There are dozens of well-documented cases on file now which include photographs of people who look more like twins, or brothers and sisters, even though they are separated by a century of time, or even race and culture. Even a man who 'comes back' as a female may still bear a remarkable resemblance!

Science has helped in other ways as well, and mostly in the realm of theory. Today, thanks to quantum mechanics and quantum theory, we have a better understanding of time and just how the universe is formed at its most fundamental level. Physicists now routinely talk about a state of 'timelessness' that exists beyond and outside our normal perception of things - and you'll see in these pages how all of this helps support the case that reincarnation is not only happening, but possible in terms of the nature of the universe itself.

Past life memories most often present themselves

spontaneously and usually in the memories and dreams of children before the age of seven. However, what has really supercharged a renewed interest in reincarnation is modern psychology and modern medicine. In recent years, some of the world's top and most respected psychiatric medical doctors - such as Dr Brian Weiss, Dr Paul DeBell and Dr Ian Stevenson - have confronted regressed memories in their patients which can have no other explanation than that of being actual cases of reincarnation.

But you don't necessarily have to understand all the deeper scientific or medical theories about how reincarnation works to appreciate the amazing case studies you will read about in this book. Every story is a very human story - about people living their lives, dying in peaceful or tragic ways - only to seemingly live again with memories of past lives still intact.

Each case of reincarnation investigation is like a voyage that changes lives and expands the perspective of those involved, and those of us who marvel at their cases.

You don't even have to be a believer to enjoy and be amazed at the cases of reincarnation you will read about here. In fact, the sceptic may enjoy this even more! That's because the confounding and tantalizing details of reincarnational cases are so strange, and so difficult to explain away, that those who consider themselves diehard rational empirical sceptics, and even atheists, will be challenged to find alternative theories about what these people report through direct experience.

It is our hope that the sceptic, the believer and those sitting on the fence alike will be challenged to think outside the box.

Dr Paul DeBell – Past Life Regression Therapy

A respected Ivy League trained psychiatrist has not only embraced past life regression as a healing tool – he believes he has been personally reincarnated more than once over thousands of years

This respected doctor's job is to help other people free themselves from delusions of the mind. Trained at one of the world's finest institutions, Cornell University Medical College in New York, Dr Paul DeBell is a psychiatrist and an expert at bringing people who are out of touch with reality back to mental health and normalcy.

So when Dr DeBell publically makes the sensational claim that he once lived another life thousands of years ago as a caveman, it would be difficult to accuse him of suffering from some kind of fantasy or psychological instability.

In an August 2010 interview with the New York Times, Dr DeBell revealed that he not only believes he lived during the Stone Age, but a number of other lives throughout history as well. For Dr DeBell reincarnation is not theory or a part of some arcane Eastern religious belief system – but fact.

Paul DeBell believes he once lived as a Tibetan monk, and also lived a life in Germany where he refused to help the Nazis take away his Jewish neighbour to the death camps.

Like many men of science and medicine, DeBell began his career as a person with only a vague sense of spirituality. He was raised in a traditional, mainstream

Protestant family. Even so, he was interested enough in religion to major in theology as an undergraduate at Oberlin University. However, as he continued to pursue his education and medical career, his religious beliefs quickly fell away. As a doctor he noticed that it tended to be the people who had no religion – even atheists – who seemed more ethical, kind and well-adjusted than those grounded in some form of organized religion.

Thus, as he advanced through medical school, it was science, not a sense of religion or a possible spiritual connection, that became his primary focus in treating his patients. He came to believe that the highly rational science of psychology was a far better tool to use in helping human beings live happier, well-adjusted lives than an appeal to some sort of higher power.

This was DeBell's focus for more than twenty years. But then one day, on a holiday trip to Rio de Janeiro, something happened to Paul that might seem like an extremely minor event to most people – a leaf fell on his head. For some subtle reason, DeBell perceived this as a sign. It was the first indication, he believes, that certain spiritual forces were attempting to get in touch with him – trying to get through to him with the message: 'There's more.'

This leaf experience led DeBell to start paying attention. It was the subtle signs that he was looking for. Because these 'messages' were so slight and ephemeral, he realized that he would have to take a disciplined and systematic approach to patching together the meaning of it all. He started to keep a log of what he believed to be the subtle signs and over a period of time, he began to notice a pattern. Some 'higher source' was trying to tell him something – trying to lead him somewhere.

Then at the age of forty, Dr De Bell decided to undergo a form of regressive hypnotherapy which would send his mind back into the distant past. The reason he decided to try it for himself was partly because of his ongoing monitoring of spiritual signs – but also that he had been using hypnotherapy with great success on many of his patients.

To his utter and complete surprise he had found that some of his patients seemed to spontaneously recall past lives while under hypnosis. They described people, lives and locations where they once lived in a distant past. These impressions garnered under hypnosis seemed extremely real and vivid for his patients.

At first Paul postulated that these people were inventing fantasies as a way to dramatize their own traumas. For example, a person suffering from a lifetime of obesity might regress to a previous lifetime where they experienced a great deal of starvation, or perhaps died as the result of famine.

Paul speculated that some kind of abnormal fantasy about having starved at some other time was a hypnotically-invented psycho-drama invented by the patient, and it was this that represented the symbolic need to overeat and remain obese.

However, what confounded Paul was the fact that many of his patients were remembering their past lives in great and vivid detail and that, in many cases, the particulars of these past lives seemed to have nothing to do with their current psychological troubles. Furthermore, the patients in many instances were able to describe specific events and facts in great detail about the times and places they seemed to regress back to – facts that simply they could not have known.

Intrigued, Paul decided to subject himself to a hypnotic past life regression session with the help of specialists at the Michael Newton Institute. He was stunned to experience extremely vivid details of not just one, but a number of previous lives. In one of his lives he said he lived in ancient times as a caveman. This life came to a tragic end. Paul told New York Times reporter Lisa Miller:

"I was going along, going along, going along, and I got eaten," he said.

Today Dr DeBell continues to practice psychiatric medicine in New York. He is among a growing cadre of fellow psychiatrists and psychologists who are embracing not only the idea that all of us have been reincarnated from past lives – but that unlocking the memories of these lives can be the key to either curing problems of mental health or helping us to become better adjusted, well-rounded and spiritual people.

The theory is that all of us have probably lived before and that whether we remember these past lives or not, they continue to exert an emotional and psychological influence on our lives today. Many times, for example, people who experienced tragic pain, a horrifying death or great loss in a previous life can carry that trauma over to their current life. It can influence the way we feel or act – but we don't know why.

Dr DeBell and others say that the uncovering of pain and trauma of previous lives and understanding that life goes on – in life after life – helps people gain a more spiritual understanding of the suffering of present day existence.

Even though past-life regression using hypnosis is controversial among psychiatric professionals today, there is a growing list of highly respected, Ivy League trained medical doctors who are embracing the idea of reincarnation as fact. The bottom line is that past-life regression therapy works and this therefore raises the very real possibility that reincarnation is more fact than fiction.

Jeffrey Keene & The Civil War General

In 2004 a front page story appeared in The Connecticut Post telling the amazing story of Jeffrey Keene – a man who could not be a more 'regular guy' and highly respected member of his local community.

For years Keene worked as a professional firefighter with the Westport Fire Department in Westport, Connecticut, and also served as its Assistant Fire Chief. During his years of service he was decorated for bravery and honoured for his years of dedication to battling fires and saving lives.

However, Jeffrey Keene didn't consider himself to be anything special. In fact he described himself as just like any other person stumbling through life, minding his own business.

But it was in 1991 that he experienced something so extraordinary that he became convinced that his life on this planet or, indeed anyone's life, was not so ordinary after all.

It was in the summer of 1991 that Jeffrey and his wife, Anna, were on vacation in Sharpsburg, Maryland. The long-married couple felt at their ease, meandering along as they searched for antiques in the numerously dotted quaint tourist shops which could be found there.

Perusing some local maps they learned that the famous American Civil War Battle of Antietam had been fought nearby in 1862 – one of the bloodiest and hard-fought conflicts of a long and agonizing war. The couple decided to visit the grounds of the Antietam battle site which is marked with a number of memorials and markers. However, it was when Jeffrey walked across a field called Sunken Road that something strange happened.

Jeffrey suddenly found himself overwhelmed with emotion – and powerfully so. Wave after wave of grief, loss and anger swept over him. Tears streamed from his eyes, his face grew flushed and hot and his heart began pounding in his chest. The onslaught of emotion was so powerful that he nearly fainted. He thought he had become suddenly seriously ill, maybe with a stroke or a pending heart attack. With some difficulty he found his way back to the car but made the decision to keep this experience to himself as what he had felt was so strange, and so unexplainable, that he didn't even want to share it with his wife, and did not want to alarm her.

After they left the Antietam Battlefield, and after some rest, Jeffrey and Anna explored a few more shops. On an impulse Jeffrey purchased a magazine, a specially expanded edition of Civil War Quarterly, which explored the story of the Battle of Antietam in depth. Jeffrey said he had never read a book on the Civil War in his life before and in fact didn't even read this publication about Antietam until a year and a half later. But when he did, an astounding chain of events began to fall into place.

Upon reading more about Antietam, Jeffrey Keene learned that in the course of the battle a general in the Confederate forces by the name of John B Gordon was severely wounded on Sunken Road, the very spot where Jeffrey had experienced his spontaneous emotional trauma. General Gordon had been shot more than six times, including once through the face, but amazingly managed to survive, even though he had almost choked on his own blood.

The book included a picture of the Civil War General,

and Jeffrey was shocked to see that it might have been a picture of himself! The resemblance was uncanny! Jeffrey told a reporter for The Connecticut Post:

"'The face was not unknown to me, I knew it well, I shave it every morning."

The resemblance between General John B Gordon and Jeffrey Keene is beyond extraordinary – but there was much more. Jeffrey quickly realized that he had a birthmark on the very same spot on his face where General Gordon was shot.

All this prompted Jeffrey to begin searching through history books to find out everything he could about the life of General Gordon. A number of other clues quickly presented themselves and a broader picture began to fall into place. The numerous similarities and synchronicities between the lives of Jeffrey Keene and John B Gordon were beyond amazing.

For example, many years earlier when Jeffrey was a young man he suddenly began experiencing severe pain in his jaw. The pain was so bad at one point that he actually made a trip to a medical emergency room. The throbbing and the aching in his jaw were so acute as to be almost debilitating. But when he was examined by doctors, they told him they couldn't find a single thing wrong with his jaw, or anything that might be causing the pain.

This strange jaw affliction event happened on 9 September 1977, Jeffrey's thirtieth birthday. It was something he had always remembered. Years later in his research on the life of General Gordon, he discovered that it was on 17 September 1862 – when General Gordon was thirty years old – that he had been shot in the face, damaging his own jaw.

Jeffrey more than just looked like General Gordon. They matched in just about every measure of physical characteristic including height, eye colour, several other birthmarks, personality traits and habits. Even their body language was the same. It was known than General Gordon tended to stand in the field with his arms crossed, something Jeffrey was known for. Both men even had similar writing styles.

Upon surviving the Civil War, General Gordon went on to a long career in politics, being elected Senator of the state of Georgia. He wrote a book about his memories of the Civil War. Some of the passages in the book were compared to the many fire reports Jeffrey had filed as part of his work as a firefighter and it was found that the word choice, the writing style and the type of specific phrases were all remarkably similar.

Once Jeffrey had discovered what he believed to be more than just a coincidental series of similarities between himself and General John B Gordon, he continued to seek additional information. At one point, Jeffrey visited a Confederate museum. One display held artifacts of a surrender ceremony which General Gordon had been a part of. One particular item was a Confederate flag which had been handed over to representatives of the victorious Union forces. Jeffrey immediately recognized that the flag on display was not the one that was actually used in the ceremony almost one hundred and fifty years ago - subsequent research proved that he was correct.

Over the next twenty years, details and similarities between Jeffrey Keene and long deceased John B Gordon have been uncovered by Jeffrey and are too numerous to mention. Jeffrey's fellow firefighters often remarked that Fireman Keene routinely displayed the command of a general on the field of battle when his crew was doing its job of fighting fires.

What many see as among the most significant aspects of the Keene story is that this is a case of reincarnation that was not prompted by, produced by, or must rest on the need for, hypnotic regression. It's a case abounding with an overwhelming amount of evidence (even though some might argue all of it is circumstantial) that when taken as a whole, makes it seem extremely unlikely that this story can be written off as an anomalous confluence.

Today Jeffrey Keene works in his retirement as a popular lecturer on the Civil War. The massive amount of research into his personal connection with the late General has made him an expert in what is still today said to be the bloodiest war in US history – when brother fought against brother and more than 600,000 lost their lives.

Jeffrey Keene now believes that losing one's life is not the end. He believes we will all live again – and that we all have lived many lives throughout the centuries – whether we know it or not.

Samuel Helander & His Uncle Pertti

When Children Claim to be Reborn: Finland's Most Well-Documented Case of Reincarnation

One of the primary ways that cases of reincarnation come to light is through children.

There have been hundreds, if not thousands, of well-documented incidents of children, sometimes as early as age two, who began to spontaneously speak about 'the person I used to be' to the stunned reaction of parents and adults. They often identify names, places and dates with uncanny accuracy - points of detail it would be simply impossible for a child so young to know.

The theory is that infants and tots have minds that are still open and uncluttered. There is a shorter period of time between their 'rebirth' and the memories of their past lives. As children grow older, the process of filling their minds with all the noise of their new environment, society and lives quickly covers up, buries and pushes aside any leftover memories they may have retained from a previous existence.

One sensational case was picked up by a number of newspapers in Finland, including the English language version of The Helsinki Times. Reincarnation is not exactly a hot topic among the practical and sober-minded Finish people, but the story of Pertti Haikio was so strange and compelling - and produced with so much tantalizing evidence - it is not difficult to understand the attention it received.

Pertti Haikio was born in 1957 in Helsinki. By all accounts he was a normal child and young man, often described as affectionate and musical. He learned to play the guitar with considerable skill and showed great talent as a teenager. His family life was somewhat troubled - his parents divorced in 1969 when he was twelve. His mother, Anneli, later remarried.

In 1975 when Pertti was eighteen, his mother was away on a cruise, where she suddenly received a strange vision as she rested in bed. Her deceased father appeared to her, stared down at her silently and simply nodded to her, then vanished. Anneli was naturally perplexed and amazed. What could be the meaning of it? It seemed to be a sign or omen of something - and perhaps it was - because on that very day, Anneli learned that her young son, Pertti, had lost his life.

Pertti had a sister named Marja. She married a man by the name of Pentti Helander. About two months after the death of her brother, Marja discovered that she was pregnant. Despite being married, the couple was not ready to bring a new child into the world and Marja was considering an abortion. But her future baby was spared thanks to a dream. Marja said that her recently deceased brother appeared to her in a dream, looked directly at her and uttered only a single phrase:

"Keep that child."

Marja decided to bring her child to term and seven months later Samuel Helander was born - the little nephew of the now deceased Pertti Haikio.

As it happened, Samuel turned out to be a remarkably intelligent and precocious child. He started speaking rather well at just age one. At one point, a relative asked the tiny tot what his name was. To everyone's astonishment, Samuel said:

"My name is Pertti!"

At first, they all tried to explain this away by saying that young Samuel was trying to say the name of his father - which was Pentti - similar to his dead uncle, Pertti. But when they tried to correct the child, he shook his head, and insisted he was not saying his father's name.

This incident may have just been passed over as the whims of an innocent child, but Samuel had more stunning comments in store that would be difficult to explain. For example, very early on he began to insist that Marja was not his mother. He preferred to call his maternal grandmother 'mother' who was of course the mother of the former Pertti.

At age two, little Samuel happened to see a photo of his Uncle Pertti. In this photograph, Pertti was in bed because of an accident he suffered on a construction site, damaging both legs. He was in double casts for five months. Samuel's remarks upon seeing the photo, which did not show Pertti's legs as they were under the sheets, were:

"This was me when my legs were ill."

Later, Samuel remarked that both his legs were in casts – something which was true of his Uncle Pertti, but which Samuel could not have known. At any rate, he was still only two years old, and most two year olds probably are not familiar with what a cast is, or what it is for.

Samuel never strayed from his insistence that he was Pertti. He generally accepted being called Samuel, but often remarked up until the age of ten that his real name was Pertti.

Samuel's parents were not particularly religious people. They were traditional mainstream Lutherans. They had heretofore never given any thought to reincarnation. Even though it seemed exceedingly odd that Samuel insisted that he was Pertti numerous times, they more or less shrugged it off - except that the little boy would occasionally drop other bombshells.

When he was five years old, for example, he made mention of the time he was severely bitten on the leg by a dog. Samuel had never been bitten by a dog, but Pertti had – at the age of five – the same age that Samuel brought forward this memory.

Samuel also had an extreme fear of water and drowning, even though he had never experienced trauma associated with water. His deceased Uncle Pertti had once nearly drowned in the bathtub as a toddler, however.

All of these incidents, incredible as they seem, might still reasonably be explained in rational ways. For example, little Samuel most likely heard his parents and family make frequent mention of his dead uncle, who died suddenly at a tragically young age. Samuel most likely also saw pictures of Pertti in family albums.

But Samuel's remarkable revelations were not nearly finished. The following example of past-life recall could have no scientific explanation.

At three years old, Samuel suddenly began talking about a time when he and his father went to a house where they both donned coloured party hats. He also said his dad had purchased a guitar at this location. Furthermore, Samuel provided an additional detail, stating that the house caught on fire, forcing him and his father to flee the residence.

Nothing like this ever happened to Samuel – but these exact events were experienced by his Uncle Pertti. About a year before Pertti had died in 1975, he went to a party at a friend's house. His father went along as well, and both father and son put on festive party hats. During the course of the party, a fire somehow broke out in the attic of the home, forcing all the party-goers to evacuate the residence.

There was simply no way Samuel could have known about this event. His mum and dad didn't know about it. They heard the facts later from Samuel's grandfather (Pertti's father who attended the party with him).

The number of specific events where Samuel was able to associate something that had belonged to Pertti or happened to him are almost too numerous to mention. A few of them include:

- After Pertti died most of his belongings were given away or disposed of except for a few items, including his beloved guitar. At age three, Samuel was playing in the closet and came out with Pertti's guitar, claiming that he had found his guitar.
- One of the items of clothing that belonged to Pertti was a corduroy jacket. It was perhaps the only item of clothing that had not been disposed of because it had been overlooked. One day Samuel's grandmother found the jacket and was discussing with Marja what to do with it. They concluded that they should give it away. Hearing this, Samuel became agitated and said:

"You can't give that jacket away! It's mine!"

- For some quirky reason Pertti had owned a watch in which both hands were broken, but he kept it and liked to wear it anyway. Samuel discovered this item while rummaging through a drawer, and retained it as one of his most valued possessions. He even tucked it under his pillow when he slept at night.
- Samuel at least twice identified the grave of his deceased uncle as his own grave. On one occasion he went with his mother to visit the grave of Pertti. Samuel became excited and said repeatedly:

"That's my grave! That's my grave!"

He did the same thing when visiting the graveyard with his grandmother on a separate occasion.

The apparent reincarnation phenomenon of Pertti Haikio to Samuel Helander was so remarkable that media reports attracted the attention of one of the world's foremost experts on reincarnation, Dr Ian Stevenson of the University of Virginia, a respected medical doctor and psychiatrist who studied and documented hundreds of cases of reincarnation over many years.

Dr Stevenson concluded that the case of Pertti Haikio and Samuel Helander was an authentic case of reincarnation – a conclusion that the parents of Samuel Helander came to accept as well, and continue to do to this day.

The Amazing Case of Uttara Huddar & Xenoglossy

Among the most intriguing phenomena associated with some cases of reincarnation is something called 'xenoglossy'. This is when a person displays the ability to speak in a language that they do not know, were never exposed to, or did not learn in the normal way.

Xenoglossy has also been associated with entirely mysterious languages never heard before. Such is the case when some Christians purport to 'speak in tongues' which resembles no known dialect and perhaps sounds like gibberish to outsiders.

There have been dozens of well-documented cases of people who claim to remember vivid details of a past life and, indeed, these people then demonstrate the ability to speak the language of their former self - even if that vernacular is completely foreign to their current culture and learning.

Such is the case of Uttara Huddar of Nagpur, India, a city of about a million residents in the central part of that country. She was born in 1941. Her parents were GM and Manoram Huddar. They were a fairly well-to-do middle class family. Mr Huddar was a graduate of Nagpur University and became a landowner and farmer.

The city of Nagpur, like most locations in India, is a rich blend of diverse ethnic peoples, languages and cultures. Several languages are spoken, including Hindi, Hindi-Urdu, Marathi and Bengali. The language of the Huddar family was Marathi. They did not speak nor could they understand Bengali – a fact which will loom large in the astounding case of Uttara Huddar.

Early Signs

Throughout her young years Uttara was a normal child by all accounts, and she displayed no overt signs or memories to indicate a person who might be reincarnated although, looking back, there were signs.

For example, as a child Uttara developed an extreme phobia to snakes but there seemed to be no apparent reason for this. The phobia was particularly pronounced between the ages of six and eight. She never encountered or was endangered by a snake in her young life. This is significant because during her pregnancy Uttara's mother experienced a repeated and vivid dream in which a cobra was threatening to bite her right toe. She would usually kick away the snake in her dream and wake up in a fright. When Uttara's reincarnated personality began to manifest itself later, the connection with this cobra from her mother's dreams would become clear.

Another childhood indication was Uttara's intense, almost unusual interest in the Bengali culture. She was fascinated with Bengali literature and read many books by Bengali authors. Even so, she never learned or read the language itself, and rather only read Marathi translations of Bengali works.

Uttara grew up and went onto a successful college career, earning two master's degrees in English and Public Administration. She advanced to a successful job working at Nagpur University. In 1979 at the age of thirty-two, Uttara suddenly became seriously ill with asthma and a gynaecological problem. To help with her recovery, Huddar adopted the practice of meditation as taught to her by a yogi she met while in the hospital.

A Doorway Opened

The practice of meditation seemed to open a doorway into Uttara's soul – it appeared to transform her into a different person – but not in the mundane sense. It seems she literally became someone else – an entirely different personality.

For example, Uttara suddenly began to speak fluent Bengali, despite never having attempted to learn the language before. She also became extremely enamoured with Bengali culture, customs and lifestyle. She began to dress in the manner of the Bengal people. It wasn't just that Uttara now could speak Bengali – it was the only language she spoke! Her own parents could often no longer communicate with her, not understanding a word she said.

Her mother and father were naturally alarmed at Uttara's strange transformation. Not only was their daughter speaking in the Bengali tongue, but there was much else about her that was odd. She seemed to be a different person, with a different personality and different mannerisms. She obviously didn't recognize her own parents. She seemed disorientated and confused. The family finally resorted to bringing in Bengali translators to speak with her in an attempt to get to the bottom of this sudden transformation from a woman of the Marathi culture to that of Bengali.

To everyone's amazement Uttara no longer felt that she was Uttara – in fact she had no idea who Uttara was - she identified herself as someone called Sharada.

In questioning the manifestation of this strange personality who seemed to be in possession of Uttara Huddar, researchers learned that the Sharada personality identified herself as someone who believed she was living in the 19th century, around the year 1840. Sharada recognized herself as a woman who lived in the West Bengal region, and that her father's name was Brajnath Chattopadhay and her mother, Renukha Devi. Sharada did not know or understand that the year was 1973. She seemed psychologically stuck in another time.

Genealogists researched the names that Sharda had identified as her parents and it was discovered that such a couple had lived in West Bengal in the 19th century and that they had a daughter named Sharada.

Sharada, now apparently speaking through Uttara Huddar, also named other relatives, including uncles, aunts, a brother, as well as other people she knew. Most of these names were verified in the genealogical records of the Bengal region, and of this family.

Reincarnation or Possession?

Before we move on with our story, it should be stated at this point that the case of Uttara Huddar is classified by some researchers as a phenomenon more akin to possession than to a case of reincarnation. That's because when Sharada would manifest her personality, no traces of Uttara could be found. It was as if Uttara receded into the background while Sharada took control of the body which hosted both personalities.

A more modern or scientific interpretation of the Uttara Huddar case might be what psychologists call split personality syndrome – except that the subsequent facts do not support a scenario either for possession or split personality. All things considered, this seems to be a powerful case for reincarnation.

When the personality of Sharada came forward, she would stay in place for days at a time, and then Uttara would return to her own self. She had absolutely no memory of what she said or did as Sharada.

World Attention

The story of Uttara Huddar was so sensational it attracted the attention of a number of regional newspapers. Stories of reincarnation are often spoken about quite freely in India, where millions of Hindu and other religions accept reincarnation as a matter of common knowledge and fact, but the extraordinary nature of this case captured the attention of some of the top experts and researchers of reincarnational issues around the world. Whenever Sharada was manifest in the body of Uttara, investigators were able to gather significant amounts of information that bolstered the credibility that this was a genuine personality from the 19th century which seemed to be speaking through a modern-day, well-educated woman.

Not surprisingly, the Sharada personality displayed ignorance and confusion about modern technology. She knew nothing about electricity, automobiles and was baffled by such items as televisions and radios. In fact, most of these things frightened her. When she heard her own voice on a tape recorder she said she believed the 'box' was infested with 'an evil spirit'.

She was also able to provide rich details of her life in 19th century West Bengal.

Sharada said that her father was a priest and that he had made an arranged marriage for her when she was seven years old. She said her mother died when she was two years old and that her father remarried a woman named Anandamoyi. She said the husband she married at the age of seven was an Ayurvedic physician named Vishwanath Mukhopadhaya.

The subject of Sharada's husband presents an intriguing side note to the story.

While Uttara was in the hospital being treated for asthma, her physician was a certain Dr Joshi. Sharada displayed an immediate attraction for Dr Joshi and acted as if she knew him. On one occasion, Sharada observed Dr Joshi in friendly conversation with another woman, which caused Sharada to become very angry. She rebuked him in a fit of jealousy for displaying so much attention to 'that other woman' in public. This caused many to theorize that Dr Joshi might have been the reincarnation of Dr Mukhopadhaya, Sharada's husband of the 19th century. The further speculation is that the recognition of her 'husband' is what triggered Sharada to come forward at this time.

It is the general belief among those who believe in reincarnation that people return in groups, and that we often find ourselves in relationships with people today that we were involved with in past lives. A connection between Dr Joshi and Dr Mukhopadhaya was never established however.

The Dream Revealed
Now let's return to that persistent dream Uttara's mother experienced during her pregnancy. She had a persistent, repeated dream that she confronted a cobra which either bit her on the right toe, or tried to do so. Sharada reported that she also had been attacked by a cobra and was bitten on the right toe, after which she became extremely ill. The last thing she remembered was being carried on a stretcher when she became unconscious – but she does not remember anything after that, including dying. This is always the last story that Sharada could

recall about her life.

Researchers noted, however, that Sharada did not believe herself to be dead, nor did she accept that she had now reincarnated as Uttara Huddar. Sharada insisted that she was alive. She said:

"I am not a spirit. I am a woman."

Sharada was frequently asked if she knew who Uttara Huddar was, and she always proclaimed to have never heard of her.

Many other fascinating side issues played out in the Uttara-Sharada case. For example, Sharada actually held people of the Marathi culture in contempt. As a Bengali, she considered anyone of Maratha variety to be of a lower class.

She could also name with extreme accuracy geographic locations of the names of towns and temples in the West Bengal region – although Uttara and her family had never visited the region. Furthermore, Sharada identified villages and obscure temples that have long since been deserted and been overgrown by jungle. She correctly stated the distances between small towns in the region.

Sharada displayed knowledge of Bengali cultural practices in very fine detail, and she adhered to them strictly. For example, she wore her hair loose, always wore a sari which partially covered her head, and went barefoot when she left the house. She applied vermillion or cinnabar to her hair in the custom of married Bengali women. She touched her forehead to the floor to greet older people. She also did not like to speak with anyone who was not Bengali, nor would she let her father or brother touch her because they were strange men to her. All of these are prescribed behaviours of 19th century Bengali woman.

Nine years - then gone

The Sharada personality manifested itself in the body of Uttara for more than nine years. Sharada would show up and stay for perhaps up to an hour or two or, at times, for longer periods. In fact, the longest manifestations of Sharada lasted forty-one days and forty-three days respectively.

Sometimes when Sharada was in control, she was helpless and listless. She was unable to feed herself and was bedridden. At other times she expressed dismay at living in a strange home in a strange land. She continued to believe that Dr Joshi was her husband, and once ran away to 'go find him'. She also once wrote a letter to her husband begging him to come and get her and 'take her home'.

In 1981, after about nine years of periodically manifesting the personality of Sharada, Uttara Huddar at last seemed to have survived the strength of this apparently deceased Bengali woman from another time. Sharada finally stopped coming back to live unhappily in modern times through a modern woman.

The reincarnation of Sharada through Uttara Huddar is one of the most vigorously studied and well-documented cases of reincarnation not just in India, but in the world. Dozens if not hundreds of minute details were investigated – an enormous amount of information given by Sharada turned out to be historically accurate, and matching what could be found in public records.

It is also a case that demonstrates some of the more rare and striking aspects of reincarnation, such as xenoglassy, but also - and more frightening to some - the possession manner of personality transfer from one body to another,

or perhaps more accurately, one soul to another body.
James Leininger & The Fallen World War 11 Pilot

One of the most airtight and minutely investigated cases of reincarnation ever documented comes to us from the state of Louisiana in the United States. The story was covered by local newspapers and also appeared in several other papers, including two in Pennsylvania, The Pittsburg Tribune Review and The Daily Courier.

A boy by the name of James Leininger was born in Lafayette to parents Bruce and Andrea Leininger. James was born in 1996 and just before the age of two, the toddler began to experience extremely vivid and frightening nightmares. The pattern was always the same; tiny James would begin to thrash around in his sleep, waving his arms and kicking his legs. He would always cry out the same thing:

"Airplane crash! On fire! Little man can't get out!"

Most children have nightmares from time to time, but for a boy not yet two years old to have a repeated nightmare about an airplane crash with a pilot burning seemed unusual, to say the least. The dreams were also extremely persistent. Over a period of four weeks, James cried out dozens of times in his sleep that a plane was crashing and someone was trapped inside, and that this person was dying a horrible death by burning.

The Leiningers had no particular relationship to airplanes. No one in the family was a pilot or worked with planes, or even worked at an airport. To the knowledge of the parents, there had never been any discussion of airplanes or crashes. The family had never taken a trip by air together. Little James did not so much as have a toy plane among his set of playthings.

Furthermore, the Leiningers were very conscientious about the kind of media and information their child was exposed to. For example, he was not allowed to watch violence on TV or be exposed to video games or comic books. They were well-educated parents who believed in creating an overall environment of quiet stability conducive to learning and proper development – although they did allow him to play with GI Joe action figures – and we will see later how this contributed significantly to the investigation that was to unfold.

So it's not surprising that after more than a month of these frightening dreams, parents Bruce and Andrea were more than a little concerned for their toddler. They sought professional psychological help for James. One of the first suggestions they received was to help the child confront his fearful dreams directly by encouraging him to talk about them. This opened the floodgates to a set of facts which launched the Leiningers on a journey of discovery they never could have imagined.

Please note however that the Leiningers were not enamoured of, or interested in, esoteric or New Age topics. They also were not particularly religious. The thought that their child might be displaying memories of a past life was simply something that would be the very last notion that would occur to either of them – although it should be said that the boy's grandmother suggested he might be experiencing past life memories, although this was not taken seriously.

In questioning young James about his dreams, they asked him if the unfortunate pilot who had crashed had a name. The boy said that the pilot's name was the same as his – James. That made sense for those looking for - or hoping for - a prosaic explanation for his nightmares.

But then James said he recalled that the 'pilot James' had a good friend named Jack Larson. James then said he remembered the type of plane which crash-landed in his dreams – a Corsair. Along with this piece of information, James suddenly remembered a word - Natoma. At this point no one was quite sure what Natoma might mean.

James' father decided to look up the word Natoma, and discovered that there had been an aircraft carrier during World War II called The USS Natoma Bay. This ship had seen duty in the Pacific Theater of the war and played a role in the famous invasion of the Japanese-held island of Iwo Jima.

Intrigued, Bruce Leininger purchased a voluminous book about the battle for Iwo Jima. This large and detailed tome contained extensive information, including photographs and maps of the region and islands. Reading the book as little James looked on, the boy suddenly grew excited when a page opened to a map of the island of Chichijima, another island in the region of Iwo Jima. He pointed at the map and cried out:

"Daddy, this is where my plane went down!"

Remember, this is a toddler barely two year old! Bruce was astonished to say the least!

His son's exclamation prompted him to dig deeper. He discovered a World War II memorial organization called The Natoma Bay Association. This was a group managed by the families, friends and veterans who had served on the Natoma Bay. He contacted the association and asked them if the Natoma had a fighter pilot by the name of Jack Larson. It did. He then also asked if there were other pilots with a first name of James – and discovered that there were, including one James M

151

Huston Jr, and that this pilot had been shot down over the Island of Chichijima.

Next, he enquired what kind of plane James Huston flew, but was told that he commanded a Wildcat, not the Corsair little James had insisted upon, according to his dreams. Still curious, Bruce made contact with the sister of James Huston. To everyone's stunned surprise Huston's sister produced a picture of her brother standing next to a Corsair. While everyone believed that all Natoma pilots flew only Wildcats, further research revealed James Huston had been one of a special elite cadre of pilots that were test-flying the Corsair in combat situations.

Please note however that this detail was little known and not written about in most historic documents. The fact that Huston's sister had a picture of her brother by a Corsair actually helped uncover the Corsair connection that few knew about – and thus, for little James to know this information seemed beyond astounding.

Even with these actual historical figures and events matching the dream memories of little James, Bruce and Andrea Leininger were far from being convinced that they had a bona fide case of reincarnation on their hands. There had to be some other explanation. Perhaps the boy had somehow seen a documentary on the history channel, or even heard a historical account of Iwo Jima from the TV while he slept, and had then incorporated the information into his subconscious mind?

However, James was not done. As we said, among James' favourite toys were his GI Joe action figures. James was often overheard to be calling them by their names – Leon, Walter and Billie. At first, they didn't make a connection between this and their son's nightmares, but one day Bruce decided to ask him why he always called his dolls by these names. The boy replied:

"Because these were the men who greeted me when I went to heaven."

Bruce Leininger called back his contact at The Natoma Bay Association and asked about men with these names, and they provided him with Lt Leon S. Conner, Ensign Walter J. Devlin and Ensign Billie R. Peeler – all of whom died in the line of duty before James Huston was shot down on Chichijima.

Eventually the sheer weight of the information James Leininger provided about the World War II pilot was too much to dismiss. Today, the Leiningers accept the idea that their son is the reincarnation of James Huston.

When James grew into his teenage years, pictures comparing him to a young James Huston revealed a resemblance between the two young men which is nothing less than extraordinary.

After a number of newspapers featured the story of James Leininger, national and world attention followed. His story was the feature of the popular ABC News programme Primetime. A Japanese television programme also produced a story about the reincarnation of James Huston to James Leininger, and even took the boy out to the island of Chichijima where James placed a wreath in honour of the fallen pilot.

Finally, James was eventually able to meet the sister of James Huston, Anne Huston Barron, who was eighty-four years old at the time the Leiningers were working on uncovering the mysteries presented by their son. As it turned out, little James was able to provide many facets of information about the Huston family which Anne

Barron confirmed as being correct. Anne was also to make many connections between her lost brother and James – including the fact that each possessed a marvellous singing voice – which no one else in the family had.

The James Leininger case for reincarnation is among the best on record, and has challenged even the most hardened sceptics to explain away all of the evidence. Best of all, getting behind the nightmares and memories of James Leininger caused his nightmares to cease, and also helped him to become a more peaceful, well-adjusted young man with an expanded perspective on his own life.

Life Between Life

There is Evidence to Suggest That Souls Take 'Side-Trips' Between Physical Reincarnations

The subject of reincarnation and the documented cases of those who have experienced it, naturally leads to an additional phenomenon attached to it. What happens, if anything, in that in-between stage between a past life and a present life?

Many intriguing clues present themselves in the recorded experiences of some of the most rigorously investigated cases. Some people who find themselves recalling past lives also recall 'going to heaven' and others report spending time in a kind of 'limbo' or what Buddhists call 'the bardo' - a transitory stage between life and death.

Such is the scenario with one of the most scientifically studied cases of reincarnation which comes to us from The Netherlands. In a report published in the professional journal, Spiegel der Parapsychologie, a Dutch boy who is identified only as Kees began describing past life memories to his parents at the age of four.

The boy proclaimed to be the reincarnation of a French soldier whose name was Armand. The soldier was most likely killed on the battlefields of World War I. Kees even pronounced the name using the proper French nasal accent on the 'r'. He described a death for Armand that was brutal and terrifying, but in amazing detail. Apparently, he had been cruelly bludgeoned to death by an enemy soldier and had received a heavy blow to the back, probably with a rifle butt. The boy said he fell face down and tried to play dead, but was then struck several more times. He remembered shaking in his death throws, and then was terrified as his heart ceased to beat.

As a result, little Kees had developed an unusual phobia over the subject of death, and even though he was a healthy young boy, he often displayed extreme anxiety about dying. But as Kees' memories continued to play out, he also described a certain intermediate period between 'when my heart stopped beating and then started beating again.'

Kees said:

"After Armand died, an angel came and took me to heaven."

Kees said the angel would take people to what he called the Big Light which he said was 'pure goodness' and, intriguingly, also referred to this source of Supreme Good as 'humour'. Kees also said that using mere words to describe what this heaven was actually like would be impossible. He said it could never be captured on a 'slide' (he meant a slide show) and could never be drawn with crayons.

But Kees did manage to describe some of the heavenly environment he experienced. For example, he said 'his place' was near an achingly lovely blue waterfall which flowed over and under a marvellous flower bed. He said there were also trees that bore fruits that were so tastefully flavoured that they were better than any mars bar and were certainly better than all of the candy in the world combined.

Kees claimed to be so blissfully happy in the land of the Big Light he had no intention of ever going back to a physical life on earth. However, a number of angelic beings insisted that he must go back, and that his time on earth was not yet done. Kees said he resisted the angels with all his might, but they were at once loving and insistent – and so back he went – and he specifically remembers feeling his heart start beating again.

You will recall in the story of James Leininger - the Louisiana boy who claimed to be reincarnated from the World War II fighter pilot James Huston – a reference being made to having 'been to heaven'. This piece of information came to light when his father asked him why he had named his GI Joe action figures Leon, Walter and Billie. James said:

"Because they are the ones that greeted me when I went to heaven."

In the subsequent investigation of the Leininger case, it was determined that Leon, Walter and Billie were the names of Huston's comrades who had been killed in action before his plane went down, ending his life.

But the intermediate location of reincarnated experiences doesn't always seem to be a blissful heaven – sometimes it can seem quite mundane, perhaps like a boring waiting room or a bus stop.

Such was the case of another Dutch person who, as a child, reported memories of spending time in a bed in a 'big white room' where she was waiting for a suitable mother for her rebirth into a new life.

Mrs Henny van Sleeuwen said that next to her bed in this room was a nun dressed in a brilliant white habit. This rather angelic nun seemed to be watching over her. The entire room was white and a radiant white glow was suffused throughout. In front of the bed was a door. Henny said she was perplexed about where she was or why she was there. She said she was unable to move. At one point, the door in front of the bed opened and in walked a young woman with small spectacles of about eighteen years of age with blonde curly hair, wearing a winter coat with large buttons.

The nun asked her if this was the woman she would like to be her mother. Henny enthusiastically agreed this to be the case.

Upon giving this approval, a long white cylinder appeared in front of her - a kind of tunnel she apparently was to plunge through to enter the womb of her new mother and begin her journey back to her next life in the physical realm. But before she was allowed to do so, she heard the voice of someone she seemed to know was The Boss. It was just a feeling that she had that the source of this unseen voice was 'the guy in charge'. The Boss seemed dubious that Henny was really ready to be born again. It asked her repeatedly:

"Are you sure you can handle this?"

It asked her if she was absolutely sure, and she insisted she was ready to go back.

As it turned out, Henny would have a difficult time in her new life. Her mother died when she was young and her father was handicapped. But before her mother had died, and when she was seven years old, Henny asked her mother if she had ever owned a winter coat with large buttons and also if she had at one time worn small spectacles. Her mother said that this was precisely the standard look she had when she was a young woman of about eighteen. Her mother was certainly surprised that Henny had come up with these small details about how she looked at that time.

It is interesting to note that the concept of reincarnation tied to an intermediate state of existence is an ancient one, and has been incorporated into some of our major world religions, especially in relation to Buddhism and the Vedic traditions. The Buddhists have long claimed intimate knowledge of this in-between realm, which they call 'the bardo' and in some traditions they describe several different levels of plains of this between-life realm. Even Catholic theology makes room for purgatory – in fact ideas about the existence of an interstitial way station were also floated by the great Greek philosopher Plato in 308 BC.

So the idea that the human soul spends time in a kind of time out in an afterlife way station has been accepted by millions for thousands of years, and modern investigations of reincarnation seem to show direct evidence that such realms do exist and serve a purpose on our multifaceted journey through a timeless universe of many lifetimes.

Split Reincarnation – One Soul, Many Lives

Can the soul split reincarnate into multiple people – can one person come back as two, or three, or more?

Many people find the concept of reincarnation difficult to accept, and so what we are going to explore now will challenge the sceptics even further. However, this subject is an aspect of reincarnation that cannot be ignored because there is much documentation and study that shows it is a valid aspect of the overall phenomenon.

It's something called split reincarnation. Simply defined, split reincarnation is when a soul appears to have animated within two different people at once – and sometimes multiple people.

In many cases, split reincarnation involves a situation wherein a fetus or baby is still gestating within the womb of the mother. For example, a woman is six months pregnant while Person A is still alive. And yet, the soul of Person A seems to enter the womb and animate the baby with his soul or essence. The person dies a short time later and is reborn in the form of that child.

But a split reincarnation can also involve a person who is living today and who is embodied with the souls of two separate individuals from the past.

Such seems to be the case of an American woman by the name of Penney Peirce. Penney appears to be the reincarnation of two people – Charles Parkhurst and Alice Cary. Furthermore, Parkhurst and Cary were both alive at the same time – their lives overlapped by twenty-nine years.

Charles Parkhurst was born in 1842 and died in 1933.
Alice Cary was born in 1820 and died in 1871.
So we can see that Charles Parkhurst and Alice Cary were both on earth at the same time from the years 1842 - 1871 – which is twenty-nine years.
And yet, Penney Peirce appears to be the reincarnation of both Parkhurst and Cary.
In brief:
Penney Peirce was born in 1949 and moved around with her family to live in many locations in the United States. She was an intelligent child who early on showed a superior ability in writing. She grew up to become skilled in graphic design, but also excelled in managerial skills, which served her well in corporate leadership positions.
However, Penney had always been intrigued by the mystical. In her spare time she practiced meditation and worked diligently to develop her skills as a clairvoyant, where once again she displayed natural ability. This in turn served her well as an author and lecturer in the exploding New Age movement that was overtaking California in the 1970s.
These connections led Penney to cross paths with a gifted psychic who, upon meeting Peirce, began describing to her in great detail her past life as a man named Charles Parkhurst. Penney was surprised because the psychic seemed to be ticking off names, dates and places of the life of Charles Parkhurst as easily as if she were reading the long-deceased man's résumé.
Certainly, any clever person who claims to be a psychic can rattle off a lot of details about a past for an eager and ready-to-believe client, but Penney's psychic reader had a reputation of integrity. Additionally, the number of

similarities between Penney and the former Charles Parkhurst were amazing – including the fact that they looked incredibly alike when photographs were found for comparison.

After this astounding reading by her psychic, Penney plunged into historical records to find out everything she could about Charles Parkhurst, whereupon she discovered dozens of similarities.

For example, both Charles and Penney were successful authors, each having published several well received books. Both considered the exploration of spirituality their life missions. Charles had been a congregational minister and held a PhD in divinity from New York University. Penney also was enamoured of theology, read voluminously on the subject and became an ordained minister in the Unity Church.

Both Charles and Penney were fascinated and proficient in their study of ancient languages. They each developed excellent skills in Latin and Greek. Both were well-versed in Egyptian hieroglyphics and Sanskrit. Charles and Penney were also extremely involved in social issues and worked for causes that benefited society, both as activists and authors. They were both something of the rabble-rouser and reformer and were passionate about improving conditions in society and making the world a better place for their fellow man. More than once Charles and Penney went out on a limb to play whistleblower and uncover facets of social injustice.

The similarities between the lives of Charles Parkhurst and Penney Peirce are too numerous to list here, but one final detail deserves mention. Penney, for her entire life, suffered a frequent nightmare in which she fell from a great height to her death. And yet, she loved to climb.

As a child, Penney more than once frightened her mother by climbing high into the trees by scaling the roof of the house, or anything else of steep vertical challenge which presented itself to the precocious child. Thus, Penney never quite understood her vivid nightmares of death by falling – since she loved to climb – it was a joy, not something to fear.

So in her subsequent investigation of the life of Charles Parkhurst, Penney discovered that he had been an avid mountaineer and rock climber! Indeed, grappling to great heights was the Reverend Parkhurst's most beloved avocation – which is ironic since he would die at an advanced age from plunging off the roof of a house.

It seems that in his later years, Charles had developed a habit of sleepwalking. In this somnambulistic state, he wandered up to the roof of his house, plunged over the edge and died from his fall – at the age of ninety-one years.

A Second Connection
As astounding as the connection seemed to be between the lives of Charles Parkhurst and Penney Peirce, the psychic who had tipped Penney off to her possible past life as a 19th century scholar and social activist had more to tell. The psychic also strongly felt that Penney Peirce embodied the soul of another individual, that of Alice Cary.

As she had done with Charles Parkhurst, Penney plunged into historical record to find out as much as she could about Alice. She discovered that she had much in common with her, including the fact that Alice had also been a prolific author.

There were other numerous 'hits' and matches as well,

but perhaps the most intriguing connection between Alice Cary and Penney Peirce was a sister.

Alice had a sister by the name of Phoebe Cary. Penney's psychic felt that Paula Peirce, the sister of Penney, was the reincarnation of Phoebe Cary.

Just as photographs showed a striking resemblance between Penney Peirce and Charles Parkhurst, Penney also bore a strong resemblance to Alice. In fact, Phoebe Cary (Alice's sibling) and Paula Peirce (Penney's sibling) also looked as if they could be sisters.

So here again we see the phenomenon of people who appear to reincarnate together, wanting to share future lives as they had done in the past.

Implications

For many people, the idea that one soul can incarnate into two people is just too much to take on board. From the viewpoint of the Western scientific, rational mindset it can be difficult enough to accept the idea that a single soul of a deceased person can transcend death and reanimate into a new life and body – but for a single soul to split reincarnate, well …

But there are ways to frame the concept that can make it seem more palatable. Think of the soul as not something that is physical, but rather composed of pure energy. As energy, a soul might better be compared to a quantum of pure light than a solid object. Now think about how when a beam of light is passed through a prism, it effortlessly splits into a rainbow of colours – multiple colours. It can just as effortlessly return to the unity of white light. A single beam of light is also split by striking a mirror.

One might also visualize the flame of a candle. Fire is

defined by physicists as 'plasma'. If you take two candle flames and join them together, the two flames seem to become one. Plasma, though it has physical structure, can seamlessly merge with another quantity of plasma to become the same body, so to speak. They meld and coexist effortlessly.

Also, we know that information can be encoded in light – that's how we are able to transmit enormous quantities of information on hair-thin fiber optic cables.

Thus, when we expand our way of thinking about just what the soul is, and how the mechanics of the soul through reincarnation might play out, the idea that one person can reincarnate as two – or several people – comes closer to within our grasp.

Finally, the idea that a soul can reincarnate into more than one individual has for centuries been incorporated into those religions which have always accepted the reincarnation of souls as 'reality'. In some traditions, there is the concept of the source soul (the primary soul identity of an individual) which has sourced out many aspects of itself to multiple individuals so that it can explore many lifetimes and learn as much as possible from an existence on the physical plane.

Whatever the reader is willing to accept will vary. At the very least, what we see in the story of Penny Peirce is that there is at least good evidence that split-reincarnation may be a reality.

The British Carl Edon & The German Heinrich Richter

In many cases of reincarnation we see not only similarities in the lives of the people involved, but also intriguing synchronicities of times, places and types of events.

In 2002 a British newspaper, The Gazette, covered the heartrending story of Middlesborough resident Carl Edon who was brutally murdered at the age of only twenty-two. He was stabbed to death by one of his fellow rail workers, Gary Vinter. Tragically, Carl left behind two small children and a fiancé, as well as grieving parents.

But why did Vinter kill his fellow train colleague? Most of the reason probably lies in the fact that Gary Vinter is simply a deeply disturbed and violent man. He was released from prison about ten years after slaying Carl Edon, only to commit murder a second time, for which he was sent back to prison for life. Recently, while in prison, Vinter attempted another murder by stabbing a fellow inmate in both eyes with a plastic knife.

However, something about Carl Edon may have set off the dangerous and paranoid Gary Vinter. Carl had already faced a lifetime of being bullied at school, and he even tried the patience of his parents. That's because he was known to insistently speak about the idea that he believed he was reincarnated from a deceased World War II Nazi airman.

Carl Edon began talking at three years old about his memories of being killed in 1942. He said he vividly recalled when his plane was being shot down over England – and crashed very near the same location at the train yard where Carl was stabbed to death in 2002. He even remembered the name of the man who he said he was in this previous life - Heinrich Richter - a twenty-four year old rear gunner on a German Dornier bomber flying missions over the UK.

But there was much more. Young Carl Edon had a pronounced birthmark on his leg. He insisted that this is where his leg had been severed when his plane crashed. Carl was able to sketch out a number of other details about Richter's life. Heinrich Richter had won the coveted German Iron Cross decoration twice and had been wounded in combat earlier in the war – all of which would be proved to be true.

It seems that it was difficult for Carl to just let rest his vivid memories of a past life, but he eventually was forced to keep it all to himself. He faced bullying in school from classmates who simply found Carl Edon's claims too bizarre. His father told him more than once that it was best if he just dropped the subject, telling his son that he too was tired of Carl's insistent desire to talk about his memories – and after all – what could come of it?

The Edon family was also not enamoured of 'spooky' ideas, for example, the possibility of reincarnation – and it probably didn't help that the subject at hand invoked the painful memories of World War II, when Nazi fighter pilots like Heinrich Richter were bombing and killing British citizens.

After Carl's horrific murder, however, local historians began to uncover facts about the case - facts which revealed so many astonishing similarities between the lives and deaths of Carl and Heinrich that it became impossible not to consider reincarnation as a scenario.

The final blow was when a picture of Heinrich Richter was obtained and compared to Carl Edon – the resemblance between the two men was so uncanny – even Edon's parents now accept as fact that their son was indeed the reincarnation of a Nazi airman killed fifty years ago.

Consider:

- Historians discovered that Heinrich Richter's plane went down into a South Bank railway very close to where Carl Edon was killed.
- Gary Vinter killed Carl after returning from Skinningrove where he and Carl had been collecting train carriages. Heinrich Richter had just bombed Skinningrove before heading to Middlesborough where he crashed in the train yard. This means both Heinrich Richter and Carl Edon made the same geographical journey on the day they both died.
- Heinrich's plane had a crew of four. The other three airmen were extricated from the wreckage after the crash and buried in 1942, but Heinrich's body was not found until after the death of Carl Edon when the remains of the plane were discovered by a construction crew. It was discovered that Heinrich's leg had been severed in the crash – just as Carl had proclaimed and exactly where Carl had his birthmark.
- Carl and Heinrich bore a profound resemblance to each other when their photographs were compared.

Especially after the photos came to light, Carl's parents, Val and Jim Edon, came to believe that their son was indeed the reincarnation of Heinrich Richter. Upon the discovery of Heinrich and his airplane in 1997, a ceremony was held to bury him, which was attended by three hundred people, including Val and Jim Edon.

The couple told The Gazette that the delayed funeral ceremony of the Nazi pilot felt strange, but also oddly comforting, as if a circle had been completed and something more permanent had finally been laid to rest.

The reincarnation of Carl Edon leaves behind many implications. For example, how is it that souls return to the same geographic locations where their previous lives played out? Does the soul know or remember certain locations on the globe? And why two deaths of tragic violence?

It is theorized that souls return again and again to life on earth to learn certain lessons, or perhaps to atone for past transgressions. Was the soul Heinrich Richter troubled by his actions as a Nazi war pilot? But, if so, what could be gained by coming back as an Englishman – only to suffer another violent death – and one that sadly leaves behind children and a grieving family?

And how is a deplorably disturbed man like Gary Vinter brought into the drama? Was he simply a tool or prop used to close the circle of 'life drama' that were the young lives of Carl and Heinrich? Remember, Richter was just twenty-four years old when he was shot down over England.

The answers to questions like these will probably never be known, but they add an element of mystery to the phenomenon of reincarnation, and leave behind the impression that our existence is not only stranger than we imagine – but stranger than we can imagine.

Suicide and Reincarnation

How Might the Decision to End Your Own Life Shape Your Eternal Destiny?

Most cultures and religions consider suicide to be among the ultimate sins. Some religions consider taking your own life a greater crime than murdering another. How then does the act of suicide affect the issue of reincarnation? Are there any cases or clues that people who killed themselves come back to live again?

The fact is, there are a number of cases. One of the best documented is the story of a German man, Ruprecht Schultz, who was born in Berlin in 1887. As we shall soon see, Ruprecht not only has an excellent case to be the reincarnation of another German man who committed suicide, but it is also a case of split reincarnation. As we explained in the incredible story of Penney Peirce, split reincarnation is a situation in which either a single soul seems to animate in two or more different individuals.

Split reincarnation can also be when a child is gestating in the womb or born just shortly before the reincarnated person dies – and yet, that newborn seems to take on or animate the soul of a person who was still alive at the time of the child's birth. Such is the case with Ruprecht Schultz, who would appear to the reincarnation of a man born in 1834.

That man was Helmut Kohler who grew to manhood in the small town of Wilhelmshaven, a seaport village on Germany's North Sea. Helmut became a businessman of some considerable success. He dealt in timber and developed a prosperous multifaceted operation that cut trees, milled the timber and shipped it to markets around the world. He also bought and sold timber as a commodity on the world market.

Helmut would often speculate. He would buy huge quantities of timber in various locations around Europe, and then using his well-developed infrastructure to sell it at a higher price he would deliver it to the buyer. His basic strategy was to buy low and sell high – and he was good at it.

But in 1887 Helmut's luck ran out. Expecting certain import fees to increase drastically in the near future, Kohler bought a large amount of lumber at an unusually high price. As events played out, both political and market forces turned against Kohler's timber acquisitions. The import fees never materialized, lumber prices plummeted on the world market and Helmut was left with a ruinously expensive load of wood.

Helmut's financial situation was so dire, he saw no way out – his financial situation was untenable so he took the only way out he felt he had left – he shot himself in the head with a pistol on 23 November 1887.

As we said, Ruprecht Schultz was also born that year in Berlin, but on 19 October, five weeks before Helmut took his own life. Yet from a very early age, young Ruprecht began exhibiting strange behaviours that would lead inevitably to the conclusion that he must be the reincarnation of Helmut Kohler.

Ruprecht was unusually depressed even as a small child. When he was just two years old, he would complain of feeling hopeless and had the habit of putting his finger to his forehead and saying:

"I shoot myself."

He did this so often his mother became alarmed and

began forbidding him to repeat the gesture. Even so, little Ruprecht developed what his mother thought was an abnormal interest in pistols. Less troublesome perhaps was the boy's extreme interest in ships. He pursued books about ships, built models and even studied shipping lanes on maps. Remember, this was in Berlin, an interior city with no seaport.

As Ruprecht grew towards manhood, the similarities between him and Helmut Kohler only grew more profound. Ruprecht was obviously an intelligent child, but showed almost no interest in his school studies. What he did find fascinating was the world of business, and coming up with schemes to make money. At eighteen years old he started his own business – a laundry service for mothers at home. With this humble idea, Ruprecht quickly built a thriving operation. By the age of twenty he was already amassing wealth and employing more than two hundred people.

Ruprecht demonstrated a natural talent in business matters despite never having taken an educational course to develop his skills. At the same time, he never seemed comfortable with his success. The more money he made and the stronger his business became, he remained ever more vigilant, sometimes staying at his office into the long hours of the night balancing his books and going over reports.

It wasn't until forces beyond his control threatened his business empire that the issue of reincarnation presented itself. Just as Helmut Kohler had been facing financial ruin in the late 1800s, it was World War II that intervened for Ruprecht Schultz in 1939. The possibility of war coming to Berlin and the ruin of Germany and its economy seemed to trigger something deeper within his consciousness.

One night as Ruprecht sat late over his books, he suddenly had a waking vision. He was not asleep or in any kind of trance state – he was in his usual, normal state of mind. He suddenly had a strong image – what he said felt like a memory – of himself dressed as a man in 18th century clothing. Like Ruprecht, the man was looking over his account books, but in this case, the books were telling him that he was ruined. The memory continued, vivid and clear, of his decision to take out a pistol and shoot himself.

This was first of a long series of what Ruprecht called 'memories' that began to stream back to him as the war wore on. He started remembering more details about his past life and started recording them in a journal. He remembered that he was once in the timber and shipping business. He recalled that he had lived in a small town in northern Germany near the sea, but could not recall the name of the village. He remembered many other fine details, such as the layout of the office he once kept, and where he kept the safe.

Ruprecht was unable to investigate his persistent and growing record of memories until after the chaos of War World II was over, and the rebuilding of Germany began. Finally, in 1952, Ruprecht was able to begin his search for the small town where he felt he had once lived in another lifetime. He did not remember the name of the town, nor could he recall what his name had been – so he began sending letters to a number of small towns in the general area of the North Sea coast. He wrote to local municipal authorities in ten cities asking for information about a man who might have owned a shipping and timber business, and who had died tragically by taking his own life.

Nine of the ten responded with replies stating that they knew of no businessman who fitted the description and background details – except one – a source in Wilhelmshaven. They responded that there had been such a case in their small city in the 1880s, and that they believed the man he was thinking of was named Kohl. Ruprecht knew he was on the right track, but he strongly felt that Kohl wasn't exactly the correct name. Further investigation proved him right – he finally located municipal records recording the life of one Helmut Kohler, the man he was now certain had been himself in a past life incarnation.

With the confirmation of the existence of Helmut Kohler, a Wilhelmshaven timber merchant, the floodgates opened for Ruprecht Schultz. He began to remember more details of his apparent past life. During his investigation, he was able to find the son of Helmut - Ludwig Kohler. Through meeting and corresponding with Ludwig, Ruprecht was able to confirm dozens of points of memory, including recognizing the photographs of Ludwig's other siblings and correctly naming them, despite never having known the family or having visited the Wilhelmshaven area before – which is about two hundred and fifty miles from Berlin.

Another curious aspect of the Kohler-Schultz reincarnation case is the synchronicity of larger events that seem to embody the life situations of people joined by an after-life connection. For example, despite all of his careful and painstaking attention to the health of his business interests, Ruprecht Schultz ended up facing financial ruin as well. This time it was something out of his control – the invasion and bombing of Berlin devastated Ruprecht's business concerns, as it did to just about all businesses in the German capital. Ruprecht's business still might have prevailed – but then Germany was split into East and West Germany, which delivered a final blow to his operation.

So here we see that despite the intuitive admonition Ruprecht seemed to absorb from a previous life experience – causing him to be extra careful with his business affairs – larger forces seemed to be at play forcing him to relive the same circumstance again – as if this was to be his life lesson yet again.

Could it be that some overarching, guiding intelligence is attempting to teach the individual reincarnating soul the true value of what it means to be alive – in this case – that material wealth is transitory, but the soul in eternal, and therein lies true wealth?

Or perhaps the issue is suicide itself. The case of Helmut Kohler may be meant to show that taking one's own life does not necessarily solve the problem you are facing in your current life. You may only be reborn again to take on the lesson again – and you may keep coming back until you finally get it right.

Maroczy (Deceased) v Korchnoi (Living) Chess Match 1985

Perhaps among the last places one might go searching for published stories of reincarnation would be in specialty journals devoted to the game of chess.

Many such publications exist for serious chess enthusiasts who pore over them searching for ways to improve their game.

But a few years ago, a story spread like wildfire through dozens of these journals worldwide. It was about a game between two of the world's most powerful chess masters – except one of them was dead when the match was played. And as we will see, this strange story took an unexpected turn and provided evidence to make a positive case for the reality of reincarnation.

The story begins in Zurich, Switzerland, with a brilliant economist, Dr Wolfgang Eisenbeiss. Wolfgang is one of the most respected international experts on economics. He is frequently published in some of the most prestigious scientific publications devoted to money matters.

As it happens, Wolfgang has an extracurricular interest in a subject that some may consider less scientific – that of psychical research, although he approached it with the same scientific rigour as he did the study of economics. Wolfgang is an active member of the Swiss Society for Psychical Research. In particular, this economics guru was intrigued with finding a way to prove that the human soul, or consciousness, survived the body after physical death.

In his association with the Psychical Society, Wolfgang

became acquainted with a professional musician by the name of Robert Rollans, a fellow Swiss citizen. Robert had an interesting ability in addition to considerable musical talent – he had a gift for mediumship, and also something called automatic writing.

Automatic writing is a long-standing practice among occultists and mystics. It involves the subject entering a trance state while holding a pen over paper. The hand then seems to be 'taken over' by an agent of the spirit world. In this way, messages 'from beyond' - generally thought to be people who have passed on – are recorded.

Wolfgang, through long association with Robert, knew him to be a person of outstanding character and credibility. He trusted him.

Wolfgang suggested to Robert that they arrange a game of chess between a past, deceased chess master of great accomplishment, and a living chess master of present time. How or why Wolfgang came up with this particular idea is not exactly known. He probably felt that the complexity of the game of chess played at a world class level would be impossible to fake - Wolfgang reasoned that if a deceased chess master could be pitted against a living chess master - well, the results would be interesting, to say the least.

It should be noted that great pains were taken to establish that the medium Robert Rollans knew nothing about chess, and in fact had never played a game in his life. Again, Wolfgang knew Robert to be honest, intelligent, sceptical, yet open-minded and trustworthy.

Next, Wolfgang's elaborate plan required that they not only find one of the world's best living chess players, but they also needed to convince this esteemed individual to go along with a very strange idea. To make a long story short, Wolfgang made inquiries through a local chess club in Zurich and, through a terrific stroke of luck, was put into contact with the Russian ex-patriot Viktor Korchnoi – who just happened to be a professional chess player and ranked 2nd in the world at the time.

Viktor had studied at the best chess academies in Moscow, played on the world stage, defeated many of the best, and had later defected to Switzerland to escape the oppressive Soviet regime. Viktor Korchnoi was approached by Wolfgang with his bizarre plan - and to everyone's stunned surprise, the Russian chess giant agreed to the match.

Next, Wolfgang gave a list to Robert of deceased chess players who had been ranked best in the world during the times they were alive. Robert's job was to attempt to establish a connection with one of these spirits if he could, and challenge him to a game of chess.

Robert was successful. Through automatic writing, a deceased individual who identified himself as the Hungarian chess master Géza Maróczy began communicating with Robert. Research showed that Géza had been ranked first in the world during thirty different months from the years 1901 to 1906. Géza Maróczy was born in 1870 and died in 1951.

Before the game could begin, however, Wolfgang wanted to establish with as much rigour as possible that the spirit who was speaking through Robert was indeed the actual Géza Maróczy. To this end, Wolfgang drew up a series of ninety-one personal questions for Robert to ask Géza, posing the kind of questions that only the deceased chess master could know. In addition, another set of thirty-one questions on different topics were also offered.

Robert was able to pass on the questions to Géza, and he

received answers to all ninety-one of the first list of personal questions. Wolfgang hired a researcher in Hungary to verify the answers. The researcher was not told the nature of the project - he was told that the information about Géza was being gathered for a possible biography being written about the former chess champion. The researcher was rigorous in checking facts, including interviewing two of Géza's surviving children, both of whom were in their eighties.

The spirit of Géza passed the test with spectacular results. Of the ninety-one questions posed, eighty-six were answered correctly - and the answers to the remaining questions could not be verified as right or wrong because the proper information could not be found. On the second list of thirty-one questions, the spirit of Géza answered them all correctly.

This aspect of the experiment was tightly controlled on multiple levels. It was supervised by one of the world's leading neuroscientists – Dr Vernon Neppe of Seattle, Washington, the founder of the Pacific Neuropsychiatric Institute. Dr Neppe is a professional of extraordinary accomplishment and enjoys a sterling reputation among his peers. He is the only medical specialist listed in five different medical subspecialties or specialties in the peer-selected book, Castle Connolly's America's Top Doctors.

In his book Reality Begins With Consciousness Vernon Neppe calculated that the odds against Robert Rollans merely faking his contact with Géza were more than two billion to one. Vernon said that the individual who answered the two lists of questions could be said to be the spirit of Géza Maróczy beyond any reasonable statistical or scientific doubt.

So the stage was set for an amazing chess match between

one of the world's leading modern chess masters, the aggressive and attacking Viktor Korchnoi, and one of the greatest of the past, the man once known as the Master of Defense, the Hungarian Géza Maróczy, deceased.

The Reincarnation Connection

Before we get to the details of how the match actually played out, let's discuss how this story sheds light on the subject of reincarnation.

As it happens, among the questions drawn up for of Géza Maróczy, one was worded this way:

What year were you incarnated on this earth?

The questioners apparently hadn't initially given thought to asking Géza about reincarnation, per se, but the way he answered the question was suggestive. He said:

"My last incarnation was in 1870."

That he had used the words 'my last incarnation' suggested that he had experienced others.

Géza was a little concerned that because he had not played chess in quite a while that his skills would be rusty but he said one of the reasons he wanted to play this game was:

"First because I also want to do something to aid mankind living on earth to become convinced that death does not end everything, but instead the mind is separated from the physical body and comes up in a new world, where individual life continues to manifest itself in a new unknown dimension."

Continuing the discussion of what life was like after death Géza said that while reincarnation is a real phenomenon, human beings of today are incapable of understanding fully how it really works. Géza suggested that reincarnation is not so much 'one life after another' as it is 'many lives all existing at once' in a kind of 'perpetual now' – suggesting that true reality is a kind of eternal moment.

Géza's comments reflect what many others have suggested about the actual nature of reincarnation – that one has to take into account a more modern view of how time, space and reality is structured. Physicists tell us that the idea that there is a past, present and a future is not necessarily the right way to model our world, but rather, that 'all time is simultaneous'. In other words, past, present and future are all enfolded into a kind of ever existent 'singularity' and that the way we think of time - that there is a past separating from the present and walled off from the future - is a kind of persistent illusion.

This more updated conception of time has profound implications for the idea of reincarnation. It may mean that if you lived once, say, in the 15th century and are living again now in the 21st century – that person who you once were so many centuries ago may not actually be dead per se, but living that life concurrently in a 15th century framework while your other life carries on here today in the present time.

The comments of Géza Maróczy would seem to support this viewpoint.

The Match

So how did the chess match turn out? Who would win – the world champion of the early 1900's or the modern day master ranked second in the world?

As it turned out, the game would take almost eight years to complete. The game began on 15th June 1985. Géza prophesied that Robert would help him play the game to its end, a statement that held true.

Géza was defeated – he resigned after forty-seven moves on 11 February 1993, after seven years and almost eight months of play. Robert himself died only nineteen days after the end of the game, on 2 March 1993.

Géza's first move was e4 to e6 – which made it clear he was opening with what is known as the 'French Defense'. Again, Géza was renowned for playing a powerful defensive game - this opening and the rest of Géza's play - channelled through the medium of Roland - was intensively analyzed, and it was determined that not only was his play at 'the level of a genius' but also one hundred percent consistent with the style of Géza when he was alive.

Viktor Korchnoi was able to defeat the deceased chess master partially because he was well versed in many of the well-known strategies of the past. Even so Viktor said at times he feared he would lose the match, but he had the advantage in that he was playing against what he called 'an old fashioned' style of defense.

The match took more than seven years because Robert was never certain when Géza would 'come across' with his next move. After Robert received the move from Viktor, he would wait until he felt an itching in his hand – which was an indicator that Géza was ready with his move.

Throughout the game, Wolfgang Eisenbeiss acted as the intermediary. Robert Rollans and Viktor Korchnoi never actually 'played' in the same room. Each move was handed to Wolfgang who kept the board of play in his residence. Viktor once remarked that he was never certain who he was playing. He said at one time that he suspected he was playing the combined efforts of the chess club in Zurich. As to whether he believed he was actually playing one of the past's greatest chess minds, Viktor said he certainly felt he was matched against 'a genius'.

Whatever the case, the amazing events of this story ended up contributing to the subject of reincarnation, providing yet another body of evidence that life doesn't end after death, but goes on, and may continue on in a way that is more exotic that we can imagine.

Dolores Jay – Suggested Reincarnation?

An Unwanted Case of 'Suggested Reincarnation' Disrupts the Life of a Humble Minister and His Wife in a Small Ohio Town.

In 1975 the Washington Post ran a story about a Mt. Orab, Ohio, couple that was too strange to ignore. The wife of a conservative Methodist minister had suddenly developed the ability to speak German, even though she had never encountered the language before at any time in her life.

Her name was Dolores Jay. Her husband, Carroll Jay, ever the kind pastor, was always looking for ways to help the members of his congregation, no matter how large or small. To this end, in the mid-1950s, he learned to do a little hypnosis. He had heard that it could be effective in relieving pain for a variety of medical conditions. Pastor Carroll Jay had occasionally achieved success in helping his parishioners with a combination of hypnosis and prayer to relieve their aches and pains.

It should be mentioned that Pastor Jay and his wife were extremely conservative in their religious views. Anything that smacked of the occult, especially something like reincarnation, was strictly outside of their accepted world view – and as we will see, their situation later landed them into some hot water among their small-town religious community.

But in the late 1960s and into 1970, Dolores developed a persistent problem with severe back pain. One day the Pastor decided to try some of his hypnosis on her to see if he could help alleviate her discomfort. Dolores was an excellent subject for hypnosis and quickly achieved a deeply relaxed, hypnotic trance state. Carroll asked his wife if her back was hurting right now.

Dolores, under hypnotic influence, replied:

"Nein." (Nein is the German form of the word No.)

Pastor Jay found this curious to say the least, and asked her why she had used the word 'nein'. His wife said something else in German which he did not understand, except that he knew it sounded like German. Well! That was unsettling, to say the least!

Finally, Carroll decided to ask:

"Who are you?"

To his considerable surprise, his wife answered:

"Ich bin Gretchen," which means, I am Gretchen.

Despite grave misgivings, Carroll and Dolores decided they simply needed to know more about what was going on. Interestingly, Dolores did not recall what she said while under hypnosis and what she said in German. The Jays decided to locate some people who could speak German and let them sit in on future sessions. As the sessions continued, Dolores proceeded to give details of whom she was as Gretchen - apparently a young girl living somewhere in Germany - but either in the distant or not so distant past - or both.

Among many aspects of the case of Dolores Jay that are curious is the fact that when she seemed to be Gretchen she would sometimes seem to be coming from the standpoint of two different time periods. Sometimes she appeared to locate herself in Germany in the late 1800s, and at other times, in the era of the great religious reformer Martin Luther, who was born in 1483 and died in 1546.

When the story appeared in The Washington Post,

Carroll and Dolores took some heat from their congregation and the community. There were whispers and suggestions that they were involved in occult activities - perhaps even being influenced by the devil. In the tiny town of Mt. Orab, population then less than two thousand, this was difficult to bear. Indeed, just a few months earlier, Pastor Jay and his wife might have held the same opinion of someone else dabbling in such areas - except these strange events were happening to them, and it didn't seem to have anything to do with Satan.

By all accounts Gretchen was a sweet, kind and honest little girl, and a long way from being a trickster. She said her full name was Gretchen Gottlieb. She had the demeanour of a youngster who was excessively polite and who only answered questions when spoken to. She seemed a well-disciplined child.

Gretchen said she lived with her father whose name was Herman and that her mother had died when she was eight years old. She provided considerable detail of her life. She said she lived in a small town called Eberwalde, and that she had no siblings. She said the village had a bakery, butcher shop, church and a college, and that she lived on Birkenstrasse Street. She even remembered the name of their part-time housekeeper, Frau Schilder.

She also mentioned the German government - the Bundesrat - which was in place in Germany from 1875 to 1900. It would seem then that Dolores Jay was perhaps the reincarnation of Gretchen Gottlieb from this time period. Gretchen said that she died at age sixteen - and that she had passed away as the result of some serious illness which gave her a tremendous headache.

And yet Gretchen also seemed to be unusually distressed

about the influences of Martin Luther, frequently calling him 'the betrayer of the people'. She also described a scene in which she was sitting on a horse led by her father. They approached a crowd of people who seemed to be forming into an angry mob - they were armed with sticks and stones. Gretchen seemed to think this troubled situation had something to do with the upheaval of the Protestant Reformation as led by Luther in the 16th century.

After the story appeared in The Washington Post, it attracted the attention of perhaps the most pre-eminent researcher of reincarnation cases, Dr Ian Stevenson, a psychiatrist of some renown at the University of Virginia. Ian himself was fluent in German and could speak with Gretchen directly when she came forward through Dolores. Dr Stevenson later travelled to Germany to see if he could locate the small town of Eberwalde, which he did, and investigated the other points of detail Gretchen had revealed.

The result was that many of the details provided by Gretchen proved correct, but others did not. Dr Stevenson also made an extremely rigorous investigation to determine if Dolores Jay might have somehow learned or picked up on the German language without remembering doing so - perhaps subconsciously - such as if she had lived around German speaking people as a child.

It was determined that Dolores had never been around anyone who spoke German. There had never been any German language books or other such items in her home as she was growing up. Indeed, she had never even seen a foreign language film. Ian Stevenson also searched the Ohio community where the Jays lived, but he was unable to locate any German speaking people within many miles of where Dolores Jay resided. Ian and other researchers therefore concluded that Dolores Jay's ability to speak German was something paranormal.

But was this a clear case of reincarnation? Dr Ian Stevenson stopped short of naming it reincarnation by calling it a case of suggested reincarnation. It was certainly a case where xenoglossy was a prominent component – but it also seemed to be a case of split-reincarnation – in which Gretchen was remembering and confusing the details of two past lives – one in 16th century Germany and the other in 19th century Germany.

Although Gretchen herself was able to say that she died at the age of sixteen, she did not seem to think of herself as dead when being questioned. In fact, a number of times she suggested that she felt she was being 'interviewed by strangers' and several times begged to be allowed to 'go home so my father does not know I am speaking with strangers.'

Thus some, including Dr Ian Stevenson, have suggested that Dolores Jay had somehow established a psychic connection with a German girl who died in the 19th century – and it was this girl who also remembered a past life from 16th century Germany. Others have called it a case of possession, while some conclude it is a case of Dolores Jay being the reincarnation of Gretchen, who in turn had lived previously three centuries earlier.

The story of the Jays has been cited in a number of other studies and books, including The Witch in the Waiting Room by Dr Robert Bobrow.

All who have investigated the case agree that Carroll and Dolores Jay have absolutely no reason to fake such a sensational situation and in fact the whole idea of reincarnation runs contrary to their fundamentalist Christian beliefs. The Jays often admitted to being frightened and unnerved by the ability of Dolores to speak German through the personality of Gretchen.

Their story remains today one of the most confounding and powerful cases of reincarnation.

The Spirit Guides

The Issue of Spirit Guides or Helper Beings Is Never Far Removed From the Discussion of Reincarnation

An issue that keeps coming up again and again among those who have investigated thousands of cases of reincarnation is the appearance of a certain third party - that of a spirit guide. Or it may be some other classification of other worldly agent who is apparently assisting the soul along its way in its reincarnational journey from body to body.

Sometimes they are deemed angels - at other times ascended masters or master spirits. Just as often they may be a bit more humble and are identified simply as helper spirits.

The idea that we all have a guardian angel is probably a near universal concept, and millions of people accept it as fact. So it's not a terrific stretch from the concept of a personal guardian angel assisting us in our daily lives to acknowledging the presence of a spirit-bound helper to guide us through the process of death and rebirth.

But these reincarnation helpers are not always angelic beings. Sometimes they are the spirits of other deceased loved ones, apparently or possibly doing double duty as spirit guides for those they know and care about. At other times, the guides are strange and exotic entities.

In many of the stories we have already documented in this book, an element of spirit guidance is evident. Take the case of Jeffrey Keene, for example, the Maryland firefighter who came to believe he was the reincarnation of the Confederate Civil War General John B Gordon.

Long before he was thrust on to the path of investigating

the man he feels he was reborn from, Jeffrey believes he was being 'pushed like a shopping cart by the spirit world' to bring about his past life memories.

Jeffrey now has no doubt it was his spirit guides that led him to a place called Sunken Road, a portion of the field where one of the greatest and bloodiest battles of the Civil War was fought - the Battle of Antietam. It was there where he experienced a dramatic breakthrough of overwhelming emotion - because it was the same location where he was shot multiple times and nearly killed in his former life.

But even so, one man's feeling that he was guided by a spirit being - no matter how overwhelming - stops well short of providing solid evidence that this kind of activity is happening in the reincarnation process. However, as the cases add up, and as more and more people recall specific memories of seeing and speaking with their spirit guides, the weight of the circumstantial evidence begins to become significant. A pattern emerges and conclusions are bound to be suggested.

Not only do people exploring their reincarnational past lives tell of seeing or speaking with spirit guides - sometimes the spirits themselves take centre stage and talk directly to researchers.

Such was the case with the brilliant and highly regarded American psychiatrist, Dr Brian Weiss, who is also a medical doctor. Brian Weiss is perhaps the foremost among those medical professionals who have come out in support of the phenomenon of reincarnation as being more than just a phenomenon - but provable fact.

Because his credentials are impressive, Dr Weiss' views on reincarnation have been taken seriously in at least some quarters of the scientific and medical communities.

Brian Weiss was Chairman of the Department of Psychiatry at the Mount Sinai Medical Center in Miami, but also still worked one-on-one with patients. This is when he stumbled upon past life regression scenarios, almost by accident.

Like many psychiatrists, Brian sometimes used hypnosis to regress patients to earlier periods of their lives, mostly in childhood, in an effort to find hidden psychological trauma that was troubling their lives. It was one patient in particular - Catherine - who truly opened the doorways for Brian in that he could no longer deny reincarnation as being an explanation.

That's because Catherine's case went well beyond mere reincarnational memories. Catherine not only gave vivid and verifiable information about past lives but at times other beings would come forward to speak through her while she was in the trance state.

What was really the clincher for Brian was that these spirit beings, speaking through his patient, were also able to tell him factual information about his own life - information his patient could never have possibly known - including the fact that he had a young son who died from a heart problem at a very early age.

When Catherine was speaking for the spirits, her voice grew husky and her body language changed. After they told Brian about his deceased son, he was beyond amazed - he was flabbergasted. There was simply no way Catherine could have known about his deceased boy. He asked Catherine who was speaking through her.

"The Masters," she whispered. "The Master Spirits tell me. They tell me I have lived eighty-six times in physical state."

Then there is the case of the Dutch boy, only identified as

Kees, who believes he is the reincarnation of a World War I French soldier who died on the battlefield. Kees reported in no uncertain terms about interaction with angelic beings whom he met in a heaven-like setting after dying. Kees recalls a certain amount of time in between incarnations in which he interacted with these spiritual beings, and these guides apparently had a direct interest in what course he would take. Kees said he liked his heavenly abode so much, he didn't want to go back, but the spirit guides insisted he do so, no matter how much he resisted. They were clearly running the show. This suggests that the spirit guides somehow know what's best for the person they are charged with guiding through life after life.

But perhaps the most mind-boggling aspect of what the spirit guides really are is that proposed by a number of researchers - that they are actually aspects of ourselves - or maybe the other people we have lived as in our other lives in the past, and even the future. This is not a new suggestion, but the idea has been revived, expanded and championed more recently by researchers, such as the great Robert Monroe, the man who coined the term OBE (out of body experience) and founder of the Monroe Institute, and acclaimed spiritualist writer Jane Roberts.

Monroe and Roberts say to think of it this way:

That everyone has a gigantic Source Soul or Oversoul. This Oversoul is like the parent for each of us, and also the parent of all of our many other reincarnational lives.

But wait a minute - how can our other 'selves' be our own guides? Were we not once them, and are they not now dead and living as us?

It can get confusing, certainly!

But it all starts to make sense when one considers the

factor of time - of what exactly time is, or isn't. Albert Einstein said that all time is an illusion. What we normally think of as time in our daily lives is merely a mental construct – a way to model our world and make sense of things. Think of our normal concept of time as merely a handy tool.

Monroe and Roberts would maintain that our Oversoul exists out there in a state of timelessness. In other words, the Oversoul is eternal. It does not come and go or live and die. Rather, the Oversoul decides to incarnate as specific individuals within time, throughout the centuries, and maintains each incarnated personality. When the incarnated soul completes its mission, so to speak, in the realm of time, the physical body dies and returns to the timeless state of the Source Soul.

To those of us living right now in the 21st century, we may think of year 1910, or 1865, or 3,000 BC as long gone and in the past. But to the Oversoul, these time periods still exist. It stands aside from them in a state of timeless eternity. This means that, in a very real sense, our past incarnations are not so much as dead but existing right now, except removed from us in time.

Yes, a person who dies in 1950 may still be reincarnated today in year 2013 - and in a sense, they would be the same individual, and both would have a common source in that the parent is the Oversoul. You still remain uniquely you now and forever, but the key is to begin opening up your conception of what your true self is, and expand your vision of just who and what you really are.

For many, the conception of a timeless Oversoul acting as a kind of grand puppet master of a number of sub-souls across a breathless expanse of centuries is an extremely difficult concept to come to terms with.

Because of the way we are programmed by our society and culture, it is much easier to think in terms of ordinary linear time, and that one soul follows another through reincarnations throughout the centuries, from past to present to future.

But the evidence for and the introduction of the concepts of spirit beings, split-reincarnations, and multiple reincarnations all point to a more complex picture - but not beyond our understanding, if we are willing to open up our minds to grasp the grandeur of what it all suggests.

Conclusion

It may be possible to pin point the modern day fascination with time travel to 1895, the year H.G. Wells published his ground-breaking novel, The Time Machine. As we have noted in this book, humankind's obsession with time is ancient, but it was the advent of modern technological devices that helped us frame the possibilities in a whole new way.

The vivid adventure of a British gentleman only identified as "The Time Traveler" is Wells' tale captured the imagination of the world. Since then, dozens of similar books and short stories followed, and feature films with time travel themes remain extremely popular. It's clear that the idea of time travel pushes our buttons in a significant way. It's an idea that is just too intriguing an idea to ignore.

What is also difficult to ignore are the real-life cases of normal everyday people reporting strange encountered with slips, shifts and spontaneous journeys in time. It is also fascinating to note that as modern physics advances – especially the new concepts falling out of quantum theory – a realization is developing to suggest that time travel may be something that is real and possible, any may already be happening.

The idea of time travel also straddles the fringe theories of New Agers all the way over to hard-nosed science. The world's greatest scientists such as Stephen Hawking and Michio Kaku, are equally enamoured with time travel as is the common man on the street. Support for the possibility that time travel is real runs across a broad spectrum of human thought. Add to this the obvious fact that the time travel is a highly entertaining concept – and you get a subject of endless fascination.

We hope readers found this book to be a fascinating and worthy contribution to time travel fact and lore. We have attempted to offer stories both from the so-called "loony fringe" to serious cases that challenge hard science. We've only scratched the surface here, of course, but that's what's terrific about the subject of time travel. It's a source of endless fascination. You don't have to be a gullible believer or a died-in-the-wool skeptic to entertain a subject that has been on the mind of man for countless millennia.

Printed in Great Britain
by Amazon